- Attracted by a glowing light near a clump of bushes, a group of boys are horrified by the discovery of a hideous, nonhuman entity.
- Under hypnosis, a New Hampshire couple recount their captivity by alien beings, who took them aboard their spaceship.
- Novelist Whitley Strieber's nighttime visits from space aliens compel him to write a book that has become a national best-seller.

Without a doubt, something's going on out there — but what?

In this captivating treatment, David Wimbish investigates the origins of visitors from outer space. Citing documentation of alien activity from centuries past up to the present, the author traces the impact the aliens have had on the lives of people who have had encounters with these beings. He is convinced that "extraterrestrial beings" are carrying out a diabolical mission: to divert people's attention away from God and their need for salvation.

David Wimbish writes, "... the most important question concerns the motivations behind these alarming visits. Are the visitors interested in setting us free from our problems? Or are they focusing on our problems to convince us that their way is our only hope for overcoming them?"

What is the connection between belief in UFOs and belief in the occult? Find out for yourself by reading *Something's Going On Out There*.

SOMETHING'S
GOING ON
OUT THERE

SOMETHING'S GOING ON OUT THERE

DAVID WIMBISH

Fleming H. Revell Company
Old Tappan, New Jersey

Unless otherwise identified, Scripture quotations in this book are from the Holy Bible, New International Version, copyright © 1973, 1978, 1984 International Bible Society. Used by permission of Zondervan Bible Publishers.

Scripture quotation marked NAS is from the New American Standard Bible, © The Lockman Foundation 1960, 1962, 1963, 1968, 1971, 1972, 1973, 1975, 1977.

Library of Congress Cataloging-in-Publication Data
Wimbish, David.
   Something's going on out there / David Wimbish.
     p. cm.
   Includes bibliographical references.
   ISBN 0-8007-5371-2
   1. Occultism—Religious aspects — Christianity — Controversial literature. 2. Unidentified flying objects. 3. Demonology. 4. Cults — United States — Controversial literature. 5. United States — Religion — 20th century.   I. Title.   II. Title: Something is going on out there.
   BR115.O3W55   1990
   261.5'1—dc20   90-36652
                                                                                  CIP

All rights reserved. No part of this publication may be reproduced, stored in a retrieval system, or transmitted in any form or by any means—electronic, mechanical, photocopy, recording, or any other—except for brief quotations in printed reviews, without the prior permission of the publisher.

Copyright © 1990 by David Wimbish
Published by the Fleming H. Revell Company
Old Tappan, New Jersey 07675
Printed in the United States of America

This book is dedicated with all my love, appreciation, and admiration to my best friend, my wife, Diane
Philippians 1:3

With special thanks to Dr. Jacques Vallee

CONTENTS

1   Something Strange Is Going On   *7*

2   Saviors From the Stars   *21*

3   A Message From Space   *33*

4   Same Old Book With a Different Cover   *61*

5   So Somebody's Lying—But Why?   *91*

6   Why Are They Here?   *117*

7   Where Are They Taking Us?   *145*

8   Who Is Lord of This Universe?   *165*

SOMETHING'S
GOING ON
OUT THERE

Chapter One

SOMETHING STRANGE IS GOING ON

It had been a lazy and uneventful summer day. Stars were beginning to twinkle, and clouds to the west were tinged with the golden fire of sunset.

A small group of boys playing softball in the street had stopped to argue whether or not to call the game on account of darkness. The team with the most runs complained that it was too dark to see the ball. The other team wanted to play another inning. As the argument raged, one of the boys suddenly pointed at the sky and shouted, "What in the world is that?"

The other kids looked skyward. A strange, orange ball with flames shooting out of it was streaking across the sky.

"It's a meteorite!" one boy yelled.

"It can't be," said another. "Not that close to the ground!"

"That thing can't be more than a couple hundred feet up!"

The argument about the baseball game gave way to one about the identity of the strange thing in the sky. The object was in plain view for a good fifteen seconds before it disappeared behind a small hill less than a quarter mile from the softball game.

"Let's go check it out!" someone suggested.

"Are you kidding? Not me!"

"What are you? Chicken?"

"I'm not chicken!"

With no one willing to live with the label of "chicken," all the boys took off in the direction of the fallen object. They walked at first, but the more they talked, the more enthusiastic they became. Soon they were running toward the hill, a neighborhood mutt close at their heels.

"What'll we do if it's a man from Mars?" one boy joked.

"I'll hit him with this baseball bat!" another answered.

The pace slowed as the boys started to climb the hill. When they reached the top, the boy who first saw the light was also the first to notice a most unpleasant odor.

"Hey, do you guys smell something?"

"Oooh, yuck. What is it?"

"Gross!"

SOMETHING STRANGE IS GOING ON

Suddenly, for no apparent reason, the little dog, who had been wagging his tail and barking playfully, stopped still in his tracks and began to growl.

The boys peered into the semidarkness trying to see what had set the dog on edge. They saw nothing, but the dog stood locked in position, with a low, menacing growl coming from his throat. Then the animal turned, tucked his tail between his legs, and went running down the hill as fast as he could go—yelping all the way.

Though frightened, the boys pushed on. Their honor and courage were at stake. As they came around a clump of bushes, they saw a strange glowing light twenty-five or thirty yards away.

As the boys tried to muster courage to go on, a twig snapped about ten feet away. When they turned to look, they saw something hideous and nonhuman. Suddenly the stench was overpowering. In one motion, the boys turned and ran for home as fast as they could go. They didn't stop until they were behind locked doors.

Later several of the boys became violently ill.

The newspapers reported that they had been victims of mass hysteria. But the boys knew better. They had come face-to-face with something from the unknown—something they never wanted to face again.

These West Virginia teenagers are not alone. Over the past forty years, hundreds of thousands of Americans have had similar experiences. Something really is going on out there, and not all of it can be explained as mass hysteria, hoaxes, or swamp gas.

SOMETHING STRANGE IS GOING ON

Two men in Niteroli, Brazil, weren't as fortunate as the American teenagers.[1] The bodies of Miguel Jose Viana and Manuel Pereira da Cruz, both electronics experts in their early thirties, were found atop a hill by a group of boys flying kites in this Rio de Janeiro suburb. Crude metal masks lying by the bodies indicated that the men were trying to shield themselves from some sort of radiation. An autopsy was inconclusive, but both men had signs of burns on their skin.

The police department started getting calls from people saying they had seen an orange-colored, egg-shaped object floating above the hill where the bodies were found. The callers said the object gave off blue rays.

In a search of Viana's house they found a book on "scientific spiritualism" with passages related to spirits, luminosity, and masks underlined. His sister told the investigators that he had spoken to her about a "secret mission."

The widow of the other victim told authorities that her husband had been a member of an occult society that had been attempting to contact entities from other planets.

Unable to determine a cause of death, the coroner, Astor de Melo, ruled that the deaths resulted from nat-

---

1. This story is told by Jacques Vallee in *Confrontations: A Scientist's Search for Alien Contact* (New York: Ballantine Books, 1990), 3–15.

ural causes and closed his files, and the police discontinued their investigation.

But two young, healthy men don't drop dead at the same time from natural causes. Nor do they carry homemade lead masks for no reason.

How and why Miguel Jose Viana and Manuel Pereira da Cruz died remains a mystery. But one thing seems certain—they died pursuing contact with alien life forms.

The movie *Close Encounters of the Third Kind* popularized the slogan "We are are not alone." And it is true. We are being watched, probed, and perhaps even manipulated by forces from outside our known physical universe. We are not alone, and we may not like it much when we find out what sort of company we have.

In 1947 Kenneth Arnold, a Seattle businessman and pilot, coined the term "flying saucers." He saw the strange aircraft from the cockpit of his private plane. Since then many others have reported strange aircraft zipping through our planet's skies.

More than half of all Americans believe that flying saucers are real, and one in ten has seen one. Witnesses come from all walks of life—farmers, schoolteachers, and even a former president of the United States, Jimmy Carter.[2]

Over the past several years, these visitors have

---

2. Harley D. Rutledge, *Project Identification* (Englewood Cliffs, N.J.: Prentice-Hall, Inc., 1981), 245.

SOMETHING STRANGE IS GOING ON

changed their tactics. They are getting consistently bolder.

In the 1950s, the early days of interest in flying saucers, several men and women claimed to have talked with people from space and even to have ridden in their spacecraft.

One of the most famous of these was George Adamski, who wrote a number of books based on his encounters with men from Venus, Mars, and several other planets.

All of Adamski's alien friends were beautiful, had long, flowing hair, and spoke incessantly of the need for love and universal harmony.

Adamski provided several photographs as proof that his stories were true. Unfortunately, most of the photographs were badly blurred. One clear photograph, said to be a spacecraft from Venus, looked suspiciously like the underside of a chicken incubator.

Some may have taken Adamski's claims seriously, but certainly their number did not include any scientists or scholars who had seriously studied the UFO phenomenon.

In the early 1960s, however, another story of a strange encounter with aliens appeared in the press, and this time it was taken more seriously.

Barney and Betty Hill were driving along a New Hampshire highway when they noticed unusual lights in the sky above them. The next thing they knew, they felt disoriented and anxious. Barney looked at his watch. It had jumped ahead by several hours. His wife

SOMETHING STRANGE IS GOING ON

looked at hers. It showed exactly the same time as his. Their Timexes had not malfunctioned identically. Several hours had elapsed in what seemed to them like a few seconds. For the next several months, the Hills were filled with dread and anxiety. Finally they turned to a psychiatrist to see if he could help them remember what had happened that night.

Under hypnosis the Hills both recalled a large, circular object landing on the highway in front of them. They were captured by alien beings, taken aboard this aircraft, and given physical examinations. Then they were made to forget what had happened, taken back to their car, and sent on their way.

The Hills' story received wide coverage in newspapers and magazines. It also caused tremendous debate. Even the man who had hypnotized them said he doubted they had really had an encounter with little men from space. He believed it had something to do with the stress the Hills felt as a racially mixed couple. Things had built up to where they had both suffered the same hallucination. In other words, a form of mass hysteria.

Some people found the therapist's explanation even more bizarre than the Hills' story. Others suggested that their doctor had planted the idea of the UFO experience in his patients' minds. The psychiatrist protested. All he had been trying to do, he said, was to get to the root of the problem bothering Betty and Barney Hill.

What really happened to Betty and Barney Hill?

SOMETHING STRANGE IS GOING ON

Had they rounded the corner of a highway in the New Hampshire night and come face-to-face with bug-eyed creatures who had come hundreds of light years from home just to get a closer look at the inhabitants of planet earth? Or had they come face-to-face with their own fears and insecurities, which they had projected into the form of men from Mars?

Betty and Barney Hill's story has remained one of the most popular in the annals of UFO experience. Their book, *The Interrupted Journey*, became a bestseller, and a movie based on their story starred James Earl Jones as Barney Hill.

Over the past few years several new accounts of encounters with beings from space, or, more accurately, from "somewhere out there," have been reported.

Many have the ring of authenticity. From all over the world, men and women are stepping forward and describing how they have come face-to-face with strange creatures who are certainly not of this earth.

But the creatures people describe today are not beautiful. They do not look at all like an artist's rendition of Jesus Christ. They look more like insects in human clothes.

Not one person who has met these beings has described the experience as enjoyable. Not one person sought such an encounter. Those who have been "visited" have expressed fear, nervousness, and a desire that the strange events would end.

George Adamski told of beings so beautiful it would melt your heart just to look at them. Today's "contactees" tell of creatures so ugly you wouldn't want to meet them in a dark alley. In fact, even if you met them in the middle of a bright, sunny afternoon, they would make your skin crawl and your stomach churn.

And yet, most of those who have come into contact with the "visitors" also have come to the conclusion that they are here for our benefit. They may scare us, but they don't mean to. Although feeling at first that they were in the presence of evil, those who have been visited have later decided they felt frightened because of their innate fears of man, not because the beings intended them any harm.

One of the most outspoken about his encounters with "whoever they are" is Whitley Strieber, the author of such horror novels as *The Hunger* and *The Wolfen*. In 1987 Strieber came out with a completely different type of book. *Communion* had been rejected by several publishing companies before it was published by William Morrow. That company's risk proved well worth it. The book shot to the top of the best-seller lists and stayed there for several weeks.

Communion might have been considered just another of Strieber's imaginative works, except for one thing: Strieber insisted that every word of his book was absolute fact. He even subtitled it *A True Story*.

In *Communion*, Strieber told of numerous encounters with weird, insectlike beings who came to him in the middle of the night. Their visits were often accompanied by strange lights in the sky, so Strieber assumed that these beings must have come to earth from outer space. They behaved as if Strieber were a specimen for them to study. Strieber always felt helpless and uneasy in their presence and angry because he felt violated.

The creatures never asked his permission to conduct their experiments on him. In fact, they never came to him in the light of day, always in the darkness, leaving him frightened, depressed, suffering from nightmares, and fearing for the safety of his wife and young son.

Strieber didn't remember these encounters on his own. He knew only that something unusual was happening to him. He was experiencing panic attacks for no apparent reason, and he felt that his life was falling apart. He remembered bits and pieces of things, like large, almond-shaped eyes staring down at him, strange voices whispering in the night, and so on. But these were only pieces of a much bigger puzzle that he couldn't put together.

Strieber became so agitated that he finally sought the help of a therapist. Like the Hills, when placed under hypnosis he started to recall the entire story. He remembered that the visitors' interest seemed to be of a medical nature. They would occasionally stick needles into his head and other parts of his body.

Strieber stuck his neck out when he went public with his stories. He could have become known as a crackpot, never again to be taken seriously as a writer or as a human being. But it didn't happen that way. Instead, he and his publisher were inundated with letters from people saying they had experienced the same thing. Hundreds wrote to say how happy they were that he had had the courage to write *Communion* because it enabled them to come forward and talk about the things that had happened to them.

Businessmen, secretaries, schoolteachers, attorneys, people from all walks of life and all parts of the United States, were telling the same type of story, describing the same type of creatures down to the smallest detail. In fact, when Strieber read some of their accounts, he was startled because they knew things he had not revealed in his book.

Shortly after *Communion* appeared, another book joined it on the best-seller lists. *Intruders*, by Budd Hopkins, told the story of one woman's numerous and rather unpleasant dealings with beings very much like the ones Strieber described.

The book also included accounts of several other similar experiences that he had personally investigated. He writes:

> There is no way for me to convey in these pages the emotional authenticity of the hundreds of letters and phone calls I've received and the interviews I've conducted over the past six or seven years of UFO research. I cannot attempt to do justice to the mystery and the pain and the confusion that I have heard from so many different people whose accounts are, at heart, so very similar.[3]

---

3. Budd Hopkins, *Intruders* (New York: Ballantine Books, 1987), 176.

SOMETHING STRANGE IS GOING ON

In 1988, Strieber came out with another book, *Transformation*, in which he explained how he expected his strange experiences to stop after the publication of *Communion*. That hadn't happened, however. In fact, the encounters had increased. The visitors began to reveal some of their secrets to him. Not only secrets about themselves, but about the entire universe as well. Strieber was still frightened in their presence, but he was trying hard to overcome that. He dedicated his new book to "those who have had the courage to be named in this book as witnesses to my experience," and followed that with a list of twenty-one names.

Strieber voluntarily underwent tests to determine if his experiences were caused by a malfunction of his brain or by hallucinations produced by some physical or mental disease. He also took a battery of lie detector tests, which he passed.

Even those who didn't believe his stories did believe that he thought he was telling the truth.

By anyone's measure, Strieber had been wildly successful with his novels. Two had been turned into motion pictures by major Hollywood studios. Despite his success, however, Strieber had remained in the background. But the release of *Communion* and *Transformation* catapulted him into the limelight. He made appearances on talk shows, usually accompanied by others who had been through similar experiences. He answered questions patiently and with humor from studio audience members and talk-show hosts, most of whom seemed sympathetic to him.

SOMETHING STRANGE IS GOING ON

Even those who couldn't quite believe his stories seemed to want to.

And why not? Reading about benign visitors from outer space makes us feel a lot better than reading about traffic fatalities and muggings in the local park.

In some situations, Strieber took on the appearance of a guru—a prophet for the New Age who had been entrusted with the message of the new gods. Instead of being greeted with ridicule and skepticism, he was met with awe and reverence.

Actually, the interest stirred by *Communion* was surprising because of the dry way in which the book was written. Strieber took a fascinating subject and made it as exciting as a technical journal. He almost seemed to downplay the matter, as if he wanted to be as clinical and detached as possible. There was nothing in the least bit sensationalistic about his writing style.

But in person, he appeared more like a fanatic intent on defending the faith. Though surprised by the acclaim his books had brought him, he was also heartened by the outpouring of support, grateful that hundreds and perhaps thousands of others had given their own testimonies in support of what he had said.

During this time it was announced that *Communion* was to be made into a motion picture. Christopher Walken, an actor who had starred in *Biloxi Blues, A View to a Kill, The Deer Hunter, The Dead Zone,* and *Brainstorm,* would portray Strieber. This wasn't going to be a low-budget movie.

In the fall of 1989, *Communion* opened to mixed

reviews. It didn't do blockbuster business, but it wasn't laughed out of town either.

In the weeks immediately preceding the movie's opening, strange news came from Moscow. Several people were present in a Moscow park when a saucer-shaped object dropped in for a landing. Not only did the UFO land in the park, but several occupants disembarked and went for a short stroll.

The story received wide attention in the American press, but Soviet authorities more or less pooh-poohed the account.

UFOs and creatures from space were on everyone's mind. They were on the front page of daily newspapers, and Dan Rather was talking about them on "The CBS Evening News."

They couldn't have been more popular if they had hired a Hollywood press agent.

Chapter Two

SAVIORS FROM THE STARS

We've got plenty of trouble on this planet of ours, and anyone who says we don't must live in a tomb.

If a visitor from another planet were to come to earth and watch one evening newscast or thumb through a daily newspaper, he'd probably decide that earth is a nice place to visit but he certainly wouldn't want to live here.

Crime, AIDS, drugs, disease, hunger, war, poverty, toxic waste—you name it, and we've got it on this planet of ours.

Over the years, we have tried many solutions to eliminate our problems, but most of them have only made things worse. And for every problem that has been solved, a new one has been created.

For instance, communism was going to bring about complete equality among people. It would eliminate both the very rich and the very poor and bring everyone into a comfortable middle area. Once that happened, the state would wither away. There would be no more need for powerful government. In reality, though, communism created totalitarian dictatorships and became a tyranny that enslaved the masses as it created a few extremely powerful leaders.

We looked to technology to give us a better standard of living, but technological progress also brought us toxic and nuclear wastes and other types of pollution.

Lyndon Johnson declared war on poverty, but more than twenty-five years later we still have thousands of homeless people sleeping on the streets of the wealthiest cities in America.

We sought to improve educational and employment opportunities as a way to eliminate crime, but violence still claims hundreds of lives in the United States every day and seems to be getting worse. Rival youth gangs wage bloody battles for control of territory and the drug trade.

We also looked to science to put an end to disease. We've poured billions of dollars into cancer research, but many thousands still die of the disease each year. We haven't conquered multiple sclerosis, cystic fibrosis, or a multitude of other diseases, and we've run into new and just-as-baffling killers, such as AIDS.

Even in the areas where we have the capability to change a bad situation, we can't seem to put aside our differences long enough to do anything about it. For example, we produce enough food to feed everyone on

SAVIORS FROM THE STARS

earth. But because of political disagreements, greed, and plain old indifference, hundreds of children still die of malnutrition each day.

All of our best efforts to find our way out of trouble have left us disappointed. And yet surely there are answers somewhere—if only we could find them. Failing that, what if there are beings somewhere in the universe who already have the answers and who will give them to us when we are ready. Certainly that would be better than continuing to beat our heads against the wall.

Suppose there is a civilization a thousand years or so more advanced than ours. It might be millions of light years from earth—but for them a trillion miles might be the perfect distance for a weekend trip. These beings are extremely intelligent. And because they are so advanced in matters of technology and science, they also are far above us in matters of the heart and soul. Not only wise, they are also loving and kind, having long ago discarded things like selfishness and greed, the remnants of our barbaric nature.

Suppose also that they inhabit a world where war hasn't been waged for hundreds of years—where crime is nothing more than an ancient curiosity, and where everyone lives in comfort and harmony.

If such beings do exist, think of all the questions they could answer about the nature of the universe; the origin of things, perhaps explaining the very nature of God Himself; whether or not there is life after death; and how to put an end to crime, disease, and poverty.

And what's more, because of the advanced nature

of their civilization and their personal evolution, we could be sure that everything they say is the absolute truth. There would be no need to question a single thing they tell us.

It certainly would be nice if they would drop in on us from outer space and give us the answers to all of our problems, wouldn't it? And wouldn't it be nice if they are already here?

Whitley Strieber believes they are. After all, he's talked to them. He's seen evidence of their power and wisdom. He says these beings want to help us deal with our fears so we can move on to new realities.

They want to share their deepest secrets with us, but they can't confront us all at once because the shock would be too much for us. Instead, they are revealing themselves to a selected few and allowing those few to carry their message to the masses. When we have put aside our old ways, our old superstitions, and perhaps even our old gods, they will reveal themselves to us more fully—and our entire civilization will take a quantum leap into the type of future we've always dreamed of having.

And so the new prophets go forward, carrying the message that a new age is about to dawn, just as the old prophets—men like John the Baptist—went about two thousand years ago, crying, "Prepare the way for the Lord" (Matthew 3:3).

People have always wondered whether there is intelligent life on other planets, and the more scientists know about the universe, the more they believe that such life exists. But if so, what form does it take? Angelic or demonic?

Attitudes about visitors from the unknown have changed dramatically. There was a time when thinking about creatures from space gave people the shivers. They anticipated monsters and demons. Today we open our arms wide in anticipation of angels or holy ones. Even if they were to appear as monsters, we would believe their hearts were good and kind and that we can't judge a space creature by its cover.

In the 1950s, movies such as *War of the Worlds*, *Invasion of the Flying Saucers*, *Invasion of the Body Snatchers*, *The Crawling Eye*, and *The Blob* were released. All of these were about visitors from space who were less than friendly. These slimy, sleazy creatures were horrible to look at, and their deeds were every bit as ugly as their faces.

But what kind of movies does Hollywood churn out today?

In *E.T.*, the sweetest, most lovable alien imaginable is stranded on earth, millions of miles from his home planet, and winds up teaching all who come into contact with him a thing or two about love.

Starman was much the same story on a more adult level. The space alien was definitely the good guy. The no-good earth guys tried to track him down so they could study him like a moth pinned to a board.

Batteries Not Included featured more lovable aliens who befriended an elderly couple and helped them save their apartment building from hooligans. *Alien Nation* spent a great deal of time dealing with the subject of prejudice against those who were different just because they came from outer space. And, going back a few years, *Close Encounters of the Third Kind* included one of the most spiritual and awe-inspiring scenes ever seen in a movie, when a breathtakingly beautiful UFO descended out of the sky, looking for all the world like the biblical description of the holy city, the New Jerusalem.

Hollywood is more likely to follow public sentiment than to shape it, so it's likely that changes in the way our motion pictures depict creatures from space reflect changes in the way we expect such creatures to be.

Is it right to think that any creature coming from space is going to be a hideous monster? Of course not.

Is it right to expect that any being that comes from space has a halo and a harp hanging in the closet back home? No. Since when has technological superiority implied spiritual superiority?

But still, if someone landed in your neighborhood in a flying saucer, told you he had come billions of miles to see you and that he knew all the deepest secrets of the universe, wouldn't you be inclined to believe him? After all, his spectacular entrance into your life would certainly make you listen closely to anything he had to say.

And yet, perhaps something would make you hold back just a little bit. Maybe you'd remember the episode from "The Twilight Zone" that featured beings from space who came to the United Nations and talked

SAVIORS FROM THE STARS

of their noble intent to help us solve all our problems. They even brought a book with them titled *How to Serve Mankind*.

They told of the beauty of their planet and agreed to take several dignitaries there to see it. In the final scene one of the American men is waiting in line to board the saucer when his secretary runs up to the aircraft. Waving the book in her hand, she yells, "We've been translating this book. *How to Serve Mankind* is a cookbook!"

The American dignitary blanches and tries to run, but it's too late. The aliens push him into their flying saucer, and the terrified secretary watches helplessly as the craft zooms into the sky, taking her boss off to be somebody's main course.

The valuable lesson of that old show still applies today: Blind faith in anyone or anything except God can be bad for the health. Someone who comes in the guise of peace and brotherhood may have his barbecue grill fired up and waiting for you!

If there are all-wise and benevolent beings among us, why don't they help us? Why don't they give us a cure for cancer? Or for AIDS? Why don't they tell us how to safely dispose of nuclear and toxic wastes? Surely they know how to live together in harmony, so why don't they at least make an attempt to usher in world peace?

The most common excuse for not doing so is that we're not yet ready to receive what they have to offer. As soon as we prove we can act civilized, they'll impart some of their vast knowledge to us. Many people who say they have been in contact with UFO beings have reported that the extraterrestrials are afraid we will use whatever they give us for evil instead of good. So until we mend our ways and quit waging war on each other, they're not going to give us the keys to life and death.

Other contactees report that the aliens don't give us too much help because it would stunt our growth. They are standing by like patient parents who want to see their children stand on their own two feet. They may give us a little assistance here and there, but most of that is done behind the scenes so as not to "spoil" us.

Others report that the UFO people will share their knowledge and their technology, but only with those who have proven themselves worthy.

What would you do if an honest-to-goodness spaceperson offered to take you to a planet that had no poverty or hunger, no disease or pain, and no aging or death? That was the deal offered to a group of senior citizens in the movie *Cocoon*. Most of them didn't have to think twice before saying yes to the deal.

Could it be that the story was based on an offer that had really been made? Some people think so. Or at least thought so. Jacques Vallee tells the following story in *Messengers of Deception*.

In the 1970s, two mysterious people, a man and a woman, began making news in the northwestern United States. They called themselves The Two and said they had come to gather "believers" who would go with them to another planet to live in peace, harmony, and joy for the next several million years.

SAVIORS FROM THE STARS

The Two went from town to town. They would rent an auditorium and invite the general public to a lecture. At each appearance, they explained who they were and why they had come to earth. Then they invited the attendees to believe and make a commitment to them.

They spoke so eloquently and convincingly that they were able to gather a number of disciples who agreed to leave everything behind to follow them. People didn't flock forward by the hundreds, but converts were found in nearly every city. The Two told their followers that their time on earth was getting short. The date for departing this planet was imminent.

And then a strange thing happened. Just before the scheduled evacuation date, The Two disappeared. They simply dropped out of sight, leaving behind dozens of disappointed and baffled believers.

Where had they gone? No one seemed to know. Most of their disciples soon came to the conclusion that they had been deceived. But even after the whole thing unraveled, some still refused to believe that The Two had been anything other than who they claimed to be.

So who were The Two? Were they a couple of ordinary con artists looking for a new way to make some money? Or were they a couple of space alien con artists taking advantage of gullible earthlings?

In the long run, it doesn't matter what happened to The Two or who they were. The important lesson is that we earth-bound folks continue to look to outer space for a savior—with or without the capital *S*.

SAVIORS FROM THE STARS

You see, we are in need of someone to "save us" in a physical sense, but that's not the real problem on our planet. Our real difficulties lie in matters of the spirit. We want to know that there is more to life than just getting out of bed in the morning and going to work. We want to know for sure that love and life truly can last forever. We would give anything if someone wiser than we are could tell us for certain that there is a spiritual reality to the universe.

It's no wonder, in a world so often touched by sorrow and pain, that The Two found people ready to believe in them.

Once upon a time, people believed in angels. They looked for eternal truths to come accompanied by a fluttering of soft, angelic wings.

But most people don't believe in angels anymore. Instead, they believe in technology. So now they look for truth to come accompanied by saucer-shaped spacecraft and mysterious lights in the sky.

That ancient Book, the Bible, tells us to beware of the devil because he can transform himself into an angel of light. But nowadays, an angel of light would make little impression. Angels are passé in the 1990s. Satan would be more successful today if he came wearing a little silver spacesuit.

The Bible also tells us that there is one God and one Savior, the Lord Jesus Christ. And if that is true, why do we need space-age saviors from the stars?

"Maybe the visitors are the gods," Strieber says. "Maybe they created us." In describing an experience with one of the strange beings, he sounds as if he is describing a divine encounter.

> This being sat down on the bedside. She seemed almost angelic to me, so pure and so full of knowledge.

Strieber recoiled at the being's suggestion to talk about death, particularly his own, so the being allowed its sleeve to touch Strieber. He described the touch "as so incredibly soft that it filled me with a peace unlike any I had ever felt before. . . . That sleeve was like an edge of heaven.[1]

What happened to Strieber through the touch of the visitor's sleeve parallels a story from the Bible.

> As Jesus was on his way, the crowds almost crushed him. And a woman was there who had been subject to bleeding for twelve years, but no one could heal her. She came up behind him and touched the edge of his cloak, and immediately her bleeding stopped.
> Luke 8:42–44

The woman experienced physical healing from the touch of Jesus' garment. Strieber experienced emotional healing from the touch of the alien being's sleeve. The question is, were both of these occurrences caused by the same loving power, or was one the genuine article and the other a counterfeit?

Strieber urges his readers to open themselves up

---

1. Whitley Strieber, *Transformation* (New York: William Morrow, 1988), 72, 73.

to the reality that the visitors are here and to try to understand who they are and what they may mean to us.

But is it our reluctance that holds us back from understanding these visitors? We're not running and hiding. We're here, living in the open. We're not sneaking into people's homes in the middle of the night. We don't stay hidden within the shadows of the night.

If these beings want to lend us a helping hand, why in the world don't they come into the broad daylight and let us know who they are and why they're here?

When Jesus Christ was born, angels appeared in the sky to tell of His birth. When Jesus made His triumphal entry into Jerusalem, He came in a public way with hundreds and perhaps thousands of supporters throwing palm branches in front of Him and yelling, "Hosanna!"

He was out in the open, publicly acknowledging who He was and why He had come. And it seems to me that this is the way it ought to be. There's something suspicious about any savior who sneaks into town under cover of darkness.

CHAPTER THREE

A MESSAGE FROM SPACE

WHAT DO YOU BELIEVE? WHY DO YOU BELIEVE IT? What would it take to get you to change those beliefs?

Are you a deeply religious person? A mystic? Or do you pride yourself on your no-nonsense scientific attitude?

Many times throughout history, "enlightened" people have attempted to throw off the shackles of religion and superstition. And yet, in every age, people seem to know, instinctively, that there is a higher power. There are forces at work in the world that are beyond the comprehension of even the best of scientific minds.

Karl Marx called religion "the opiate of the people," and the Communist societies based on his theories have gone to tremendous lengths to eradicate all traces of faith. We know today that all of those efforts have failed, and that a high percentage of those in Communist countries still profess religious faith despite years of the worst sort of oppression.

People know there is something they should believe in, even if they're not always sure exactly what or who it is. In fact, they often want so hard to believe that they are susceptible to all sorts of deception.

Many who have become involved in UFO research over the years have been guilty of "wanting to believe" so badly that they jumped on any evidence that supported claims of sightings, encounters with spacemen, and so on, and have completely turned away from any evidence that would discredit such claims. A gullible public shows its willingness to believe by gobbling up poorly researched and undocumented books telling of such encounters.

For instance, for more than twenty years, the story has been circulating that the first Americans to visit the moon took photographs of spaceships they saw there and that our astronauts found huge underground installations that had been there for many years. Official sources have told us that our moon is lifeless, but some groups continue to believe that it's a busy way station for space people zipping from planet to planet.

NASA denied that any such encounters occurred. But those who didn't want to believe NASA produced "top secret" transcripts of conversations that took place between the startled astronauts and mission control in Houston.

NASA officials countered by releasing official transcripts showing that there were no such conversations.

"Ah," cried the believers, "it's a conspiracy. NASA officials have doctored the transcripts. They've even gone so far as to censor the original audio tapes."

Again NASA officials countered. They had no reason to alter the tapes. What would be their purpose? NASA's goal is to unlock the mysteries of space—not to hide them from anyone.

But it's hard to combat charges of conspiracy, especially when there's nothing you can do to prove you didn't censor transcripts and alter audio tapes. The burden of proof is on the huge government agency—and most of us are inclined to believe the little guys instead of the powerful bureaucrats. And so the stories persist.

Another case occurred in 1973 when two fishermen in Pascagoula, Mississippi, encountered some strange-looking humanoid creatures that levitated them into a saucer-shaped spacecraft. One of the witnesses, a man named Charles Hickson, had just been fired from his job and had filed for bankruptcy. Following his encounter with the UFO he hired a press agent, who produced a polygraph test purporting to prove that his client was telling the truth. Yet when neutral parties offered Hickson a chance to take another polygraph test, he declined.

Hickson failed to get a book and movie deal for his experience, but his story has become one of the great legends of UFOlogy.

Two years later, an Arizona woodcutter named Travis Walton encountered aliens who "zapped him" with some kind of ray, rendering him unable to move.

They took him aboard their flying saucer and flew him to a UFO base. A few days later he returned, dazed and confused, telling of his strange encounter with creatures from space.

Several investigators interviewed the young man and concluded that he was telling the truth. But when a tabloid newspaper gave him a polygraph test, he flunked it. The man who ran the test said Walton had made several attempts at "gross deception." The tester concluded that Walton's story was a fib.

Some UFO researchers dropped their interest in Walton. One particular group went so far as to suggest that his experience had more to do with drugs than with aliens from space. But others remained unconvinced. They hired another, and less experienced, polygraph operator to retest Travis Walton. This time he passed. His story has been given the seal of approval by many UFO buffs, even though the account is questionable and lacks any physical evidence to support it.

In *UFOs and Outer Space Mysteries*, author James Oberg tells of a hoax that went too far.

Tom Monteleone, a student at the University of Maryland, was listening to a radio talk show. A guest was telling about his encounter with creatures from space who had taken him to visit their planet, Lanulos.

For the fun of it, Monteleone called the radio station and claimed that he too had been taken to Lanulos.

The "contactee," Woodrow Derenberger, was initially dumbfounded but quickly regained his composure and agreed with all of Monteleone's descriptions of the planet Lanulos, even details which contradicted things Derenberger had just disclosed on the radio show. After fifteen minutes the college student hung up and enjoyed a good laugh with his roommates—until the phone rang. The radio station had traced his call and now wanted more details.[1]

Instead of telling the truth, Monteleone insisted that his story was true. He was having a good time and figured he'd see how far this thing would go. For the next several months, he was often asked to talk about his experiences on Lanulos. He told his audiences he had never had any interest in UFOs and hadn't read any books on the subject. Since much of what he said corroborated earlier UFO stories, those who interviewed him were impressed. His case appeared to be authentic. The researchers never bothered to check the facts.

The fraud didn't unravel for eleven years, when Monteleone decided he had had enough and wanted to come clean. In May 1979, he admitted to *Omni Magazine* that the whole thing had been a lie. He admitted that he had lied about never having read any books about UFOs and said his information came from what he had heard Derenberger say plus information he quickly gathered from several books. No wonder his story

---

1. James E. Oberg, *UFOs and Outer Space Mysteries* (Norfolk, Va.: Donning Press, 1982), 106.

backed other accounts; he was using those other accounts to piece together his own story!

He explained in the magazine how he had kept things going for so long: "I not only repeated my false experiences but also added further embellishments and absurdities—just to see how far I could carry the hoax before being discredited."[2]

In a hypnosis session, arranged by those who wanted to know if his story was true, he had merely pretended to go into a hypnotic trance—and none of the experts could tell the difference.

Those who had invested time and energy into investigating Monteleone reacted to his recantation with a great deal of anger. And some refused to believe he had never been to Lanulos. They charged that he was simply tired of being in the spotlight and the only way for him to get rid of his celebrity status and get back to a normal way of life was to deny the experience.

Am I saying, then, that all of these accounts of visitations by strange beings during the night are cut out of the same piece of cloth as Tom Monteleone's trip to Lanulos?

No, not at all.

The presence of the counterfeit does not deny the existence of the authentic.

The point is that research into UFOs and paranor-

---

2. Oberg, *UFOs and Outer Space Mysteries*, 106. See also Karl T. Pflock. "Anatomy of a UFO Hoax." *Fate Magazine* (Nov. 1980), 40.

A MESSAGE FROM SPACE

mal experiences has very often been susceptible to overactive imaginations and outright fabrications. But sooner or later the phony stories begin to unravel. Charlatans and phonies abound, but their presence should never be allowed to obscure the fact that something real is happening.

[handwritten margin note: Like religion also]

The solution is to be open-minded about such experiences without being flat-out gullible, and to be discerning and critical without being too cynical—and that's a pretty hard line to walk. Most people lean in one direction or the other. Unfortunately, too many Americans lean in the direction of gullibility.

There are those who put on flowing robes and claim to be ambassadors from Lanulos or even from Venus. There are others who speak in affected voices and tell us they are the spokesmen for spirits tens of thousands of years old. Phonies and frauds are everywhere.

There are others who have suffered irrefutable psychological trauma and have begun to look within to understand what has happened to them. Somewhere along the way many of them were transformed from seekers to apostles. There is something compelling about those who have suffered through experiences that have left them in emotional tatters, trying to sew the pieces of their lives together again.

The Apostle Paul was a zealous Jew who hated Christians with all his heart. On his way to Damascus to persecute the Christians, a bright light from heaven shone down on him, and he heard the voice of Jesus telling him to stop what he was doing. Paul, the man who hated everything the Christian church stood for, suddenly became its most ardent and powerful spokesman.

Like the Apostle Paul, Whitley Strieber has had his Damascus Road experience, and now it seems he won't be satisfied until we have all heard him tell us of this "new" gospel. Not only heard, in fact, but believed.

But what exactly is this new gospel, and how does it differ from the old one? And an even more important question: Which do we believe when the "new" gospel conflicts with the "old" one? And make no mistake about that. They are in direct conflict.

In 1953, Gray Barker wrote a terrifying book called *They Knew Too Much About Flying Saucers*. It wasn't the sort of book you'd keep on your nightstand to read if you couldn't fall asleep. Reading a few pages late at night was like drinking several cups of strong coffee. It told of encounters with strange, evil-looking beings that floated instead of walked, of strange noises in the night, and of mysterious men in black who did everything possible to shut down serious investigation into the flying saucer mystery.

Barker had spent many years investigating stories of the unexplained, especially in regard to Unidentified Flying Objects. One of Barker's friends, Al Bender, was passionate about the UFO mystery. He headed an organization and published a magazine aimed at finding out the truth behind the saucers. But overnight, Bender's enthusiasm completely disappeared. In fact, it completely reversed itself. Not only was he no longer interested in talking about the mystery of the saucers, he was even afraid to talk about it.

He disbanded his organization, suspended publication of his magazine, and attempted to break off contact with his fellow researchers.

Bender wasn't the only one this happened to. Several more of Barker's friends and colleagues suddenly lost interest in the saucers. And all of them had just previously announced they had stumbled across something important and soon would be making a statement about it. Instead they started giving friendly advice to find another area of interest.

Apparently anyone who looked too far into these mysteries was getting into deep trouble.

Barker's book had all of the elements of a first-class mystery novel, but he swore that every word was true.

Several years later Bender decided to tell what had happened to him. With Barker's help, he published a book called *Flying Saucers and the Three Men*, in which he revealed why he had given up his investigation.

He had been subjected to a series of strange paranormal experiences that had left him drained and frightened. He had heard rappings on the walls of his house late at night and footsteps walking across his bedroom floor when no one was there. On several occasions, he even saw shoes walking across the floor with no one wearing them. There wasn't a haunted house in the world with more going on inside it—and Al Bender was terrorized.

A MESSAGE FROM SPACE

Finally, three men dressed in black visited him and claimed responsibility for Bender's nightmarish experiences. They had come to earth from a distant planet to extract a special mineral from our sea water, they explained. We knew nothing about this mineral, but it was essential to them, and that was all they cared about.

They simply wanted to get as much of their precious cargo as they could. Then they would leave us alone and head back into the stars. They wanted to do their job as quickly and as quietly as possible. For that reason, they wanted Bender to stop all of his research into the saucers. If he didn't, well, he would be sorry.

They were kind enough, though, to give Al Bender some of the benefit of their knowledge. For instance, they told him they were responsible for supernatural or paranormal activity on earth. It wasn't the dead who spoke through the spirit medium—it was these people from space. It wasn't ghosts who made strange noises in the night. It was these folks from a distant star having a little fun with us. And anyone who heard an audible voice speaking from out of nowhere wasn't hearing God or one of His angels. It too was one of these visitors from space.

In short, they were responsible for just about every strange or unexplained thing happening on this planet of ours.

They never fully explained their reasons for doing all of these things, but part of it seemed to be to throw us off the trail. They didn't want us to know they were here. (If that was true, why didn't they keep as quiet as

A MESSAGE FROM SPACE

possible and not harass Al Bender?) The second reason, apparently, was just to have a little fun. After all, they were some trillions of miles from home and didn't have anything better to do on a Saturday night.

They also answered some of Al Bender's deepest questions.

Was there life after death?

Not that they knew of.

Was there a God in heaven?

No. At least not as we conceive of Him.

Who was Jesus Christ?

Merely a man . . . a man who believed with all of His being in the God of Israel. A good man, they said, one who tried to bring justice and kindness into a brutal world, but He had paid with His life. The resurrection, they said, was just a story thought up by His followers who either couldn't bear to face the truth that He was dead or wanted to use His death as a means to bring about the reforms He had sought.

Bender's book didn't receive a great deal of fanfare, nor did it sell thousands of copies. It was largely ignored. *They Knew Too Much About Flying Saucers* had set up such a mystery that the "truth" in the second book was disappointing. It was more fun wondering about the mystery than reading the solution.

Flying Saucers and the Three Men was either ignored or dismissed as nonsense by most serious UFO investigators. And it would be tempting to think that Bender had set up the entire mystery just to sell a book, except for two things:

1. *He waited too long to publish his second book.* Several years passed between the publication dates of Barker's and Bender's books—and Barker's book sold at a pretty fast clip. If Bender was only interested in getting rich from telling his story he wouldn't have waited so long. He would have followed the old advice to "strike while the iron is hot."

2. *Al Bender disagreed with what the men told him.* After hearing their answer to his questions about God and Jesus Christ, Bender said he couldn't believe them when it came to these areas. If he had been making up the story and following his own inclinations it seems likely that he would have had the space beings reassure him that Jesus Christ is, in fact, the Son of God who sits at the right hand of the Father—as it says in the Bible.

Many people make the mistake of thinking that anyone who demonstrates "supernatural" powers or advanced technology knows everything there is to know about spiritual things. But why? Just because another being comes from zillions of miles away doesn't mean he knows all of the deepest secrets of the universe. And if he does know them, how do we know he will tell us the truth? What if he lies?

Time has proven that Bender's "friends" lied to him in other matters. For instance, they told him they would be leaving this planet within a few years. That was why he felt free to tell his story. The threat to his safety no longer existed. Once they left the earth, they didn't care who knew about them. It would be too late to disrupt their important operations.

But they didn't leave. The strange, middle-of-the-night experiences that wreaked havoc on the psyche of Al Bender are still going on.

Bender also got the impression from his space friends that the United States government knew about their presence here. Nobody wanted to say anything because it might precipitate a general panic, but once the visitors left, the government would tell us all about them. That was more than twenty years ago, and the government hasn't said a word.

There is one major difference between the goblins encountered by Al Bender and the strange creatures who became a part of Whitley Strieber's life. Whereas Bender's "friends" told him they did not believe in life after death, Strieber's visitors are quite sure it exists. They have had much to say about the existence of the soul apart from the physical body, and have given instructions in the art of soul travel.

But where both sets of space travelers agree is that neither accepts the God of the Bible as Lord nor Jesus Christ as His Son.

We cannot believe Jesus *and* the visitors because their claims contradict one another. There is no way to reconcile the two. If Jesus is who He claimed to be, the visitors cannot be who they claim to be.

The visitors are perfectly in tune with what has become known as "New Age" religion—Eastern mysticism, astral projection, the harmonic convergence, and so on. They are not at all in harmony, though, with Jesus Christ, who said, "I am the way, the truth, and the life."

At the very least, they are more interested in steering us away from the truth of the Bible than toward it. Even though they deny the validity of the biblical message, however, they go to great lengths to copy certain portions of it.

For instance, the New Testament teaches that Christ died as a sacrifice for our sins—that He took upon His body the punishment we all deserve. The four gospels—Matthew, Mark, Luke, and John—vividly portray the events leading up to Christ's death. He was severely beaten by the Roman guard. He was blindfolded and made to stand while Roman soldiers took turns hitting Him in the face and asking Him to "prophesy" who hit Him. He was spat upon and had a "crown" made of thorns pushed onto His brow. Then He was forced to carry His cross to a place called Golgotha, where He was crucified between two thieves. Not only does the Bible teach that He was receiving the punishment that you and I deserve, but the Old Testament prophet Isaiah tells us that "the punishment that brought us peace was upon him, and by his wounds we were healed" (Isaiah 53:5).

Nearly two thousand years later, the visitors treated Whitley Strieber to a front-row seat at a similar event. An innocent man—albeit not Christ—was being beaten because he had failed to get Strieber to "obey" him. Even though the aliens kept whispering in Strieber's ear that he was seeing a vision and that nobody was really being hurt, he was "shocked to the core.... My heart was sick for the poor man in front of me," he wrote.

"I went through hell watching that poor man suffer for me. I have never felt such raw humiliation and guilt. I would have done anything to trade places with him. But they beat him until he was a slumped broken ruin."

But that wasn't the worst of it. Suddenly his ears were filled with the terrified screams of his small son coming from the bedroom down the hall. Strieber couldn't move. The visitor said, "He is being punished for your transgression."

Suddenly, everything changed. The visitors were gone. The screaming stopped. Strieber started to jump out of bed and run into his son's room, but felt as if he had been slapped across the face. He fell back into bed. The next thing he knew, the morning sun was streaming through the curtains.

He got up and ran into his son's room. Except for being uncovered, the child was fine.

That's quite a switch on the story of Jesus. The Bible says that God Himself became a man and took the punishment of all humanity by allowing Himself to be beaten and crucified. He bore the punishment for our disobedience. The visitors' variation is to say, "If you don't obey, we'll get a perfect stranger and beat him half to death in front of your eyes. And then we'll threaten the safety of your child."

But it is striking how closely the visitors copied the biblical theme of an innocent third party suffering for the sins of another. There is no getting around the idea that for some reason they were counterfeiting the Gospel story.

Were they interested in establishing the idea that there was nothing unique about the sufferings Christ went through? Do they realize that the only way to increase their influence in this world is to diminish the influence of Christ?

Strieber wrote: "They [the visitors] have caused me to slough off my old view of the world like the dismal skin that it was and seek a completely new vision of this magnificent, mysterious, and fiercely alive universe."

Strieber was raised in the Roman Catholic church and even attended a church-related elementary school, where—as in all Catholic schools of the 1950s—one of the most important parts of the curriculum was the catechism. One would assume that at one time he believed in the God of the Bible and that the universe was created by that God.

The visitors want to help us "slough off" those old views of both God and His universe.

People today are easily convinced that they don't need God because they have "the visitors." But is it a fair exchange—dropping the hand of a loving, self-sacrificing God to take hold of the hand of an insectlike creature that won't make a move outside the cover of darkness?

CHILDREN OF GOD?

From the pages of the Bible many concepts are being borrowed and distorted by the visitors. For instance, Jesus Christ Himself said that He was "not of this world," but that He had "come down from above," signifying that He was of heavenly origin. But many now believe that Jesus Christ was an alien from space. Far from being the unique Son of God, they say He was one of many who have come here over the centuries to help us—only we treated Him much rougher than we have the other aliens who have walked among us.

Some even teach that Jesus continues to pilot His spacecraft throughout the universe, but that He refuses to come within a million light years of the earth after what we did to Him the last time He was here.

After all, they say, the Book of Acts teaches that Jesus ended His stay on earth by ascending into heaven until a cloud hid Him from His followers' sight. Jesus Himself told His disciples that when He returns to the earth, it will be "on the clouds of the sky, with power and great glory" (Matthew 24:30). Could it be that the "clouds" in these passages aren't clouds at all, but spacecraft from a distant planet?

A few years back, books that tried to prove our civilization had been seeded and guided in its development by forces from outer space generated a great deal of excitement. *Chariots of the Gods* by Erich Von Daniken insisted that Moses was in direct contact with beings from space. After all, on their journey out of Egypt toward the Promised Land, the Israelites were led by a cloud of smoke by day and a pillar of fire by night. Von Daniken went to great lengths to prove that the Israelites were following a flying saucer. During the day, the gray disk floating through the sky resembled smoke, but at night, when its lights were on, it became fire. He also had a lot to say about the Ark of the Covenant, the chest built by Moses according to instructions from God, which contained several of the most important items signifying the special covenant God had made between Himself and the Israelite nation. The Ark was placed within the tabernacle, the "portable" temple that went wherever the Israelites went. And whenever Moses needed to talk directly with God, he went into the tabernacle. Putting "two and two" together, Von Daniken concluded that the Ark of the Covenant was a transmitter that allowed Moses to communicate with the beings inside the spaceship. He even discussed the instructions for building the ark—which are recorded in Exodus 25—and said they back up his contention that the entire thing was some sort of transmitter/receiver.

It was all nonsense, as any electronics expert could tell you, but that didn't stop thousands of people from believing it, nor did it prevent Von Daniken from selling a million or so copies of his book.

Von Daniken also got tremendous mileage out of Bible passages like 2 Samuel 6:6, 7: "When they came to the threshing floor of Nacon, Uzzah reached out and took hold of the ark of God, because the oxen stumbled. The Lord's anger burned against Uzzah because of his irreverent act; therefore God struck him down and he died there beside the ark of God."

According to Von Daniken, a tremendous current of power flowed out of that thing, and when poor Uzzah reached up to touch it, he might as well have been grabbing hold of a high-voltage wire.

How can so many people who find it hard to take the Bible at face value, rush to believe an incredible story like the one Von Daniken wrote?

Another biblical concept that the visitors seem anxious to reexplain is the idea that there are "children of God" on this planet of ours.

The Apostle John says, "How great is the love the Father has lavished on us, that we should be called children of God! And that is what we are! The reason the world does not know us is that it did not know him. Dear friends, now we are children of God, and what we will be has not yet been made known" (1 John 3:1, 2).

His teaching is clear: We become children of God through faith in Christ.

But the visitors smile patiently and explain, once again, that John got it all wrong. Yes, there are children of God among us, and you may even be one without knowing it, but this has nothing to do with anything spiritual. The children of God have been produced through the intermingling of people from space and people from earth. This "crossbreeding" has been going on for years, but it has been occurring more in recent years, they say. By intermingling with us, the visitors are improving our species and giving us the children who will be the great leaders of tomorrow—men and women who will take us into the utopian age we have always dreamed of.

Brad Steiger has written several books on UFOs and other unexplained phenomena. In his book *The UFO Abductors*, he explains that his interest in such phenomena dates back to when he was a four-year-old growing up near the small town of Bode, Iowa.

One October night, Steiger heard the crunch of leaves outside his bedroom window followed by the sound of something being dragged across the ground. The Steigers' farm was two miles from town, so young Brad wasn't used to hearing such noises, especially late at night. He got out of bed, went to the window, and looked out into the yard.

He saw a strange little man with pointed ears on the top of his large, round skull. He had dragged a tin pail to the kitchen window, turned it upside down, and was standing on it, trying to peek through the window to spy on Steiger's parents.

The little man, perhaps sensing that he was being watched, turned to look at Steiger from a distance of no more than seven feet. "Although we were physically separated by the windowpane, the transparent barrier did nothing to refract the tingle of shock and surprise that I received from those enormous, slanted eyes with their vertical, reptilian pupils," Steiger wrote.[3]

The "shock and surprise" didn't last very long. As he looked into those eyes, the pupils seemed to grow larger and larger. And as they did, young Brad Steiger grew calmer and more peaceful—and then suddenly it was morning.

That was all there was to the story—until 1987.

---

3. Brad Steiger, *The UFO Abductors* (New York: Berkley Books, 1988), 146.

Steiger was attending an art show in Sedona, Arizona, and came across a portrait of the little man he had seen forty-seven years earlier. There was no mistaking that face or those eyes.

The artist, Luis Romero, had drawn the portrait based on a description given to him by Sharon Reed, a woman who had grown up in West Bend, Iowa, just a few miles from Bode.

Steiger contacted Reed and found out that she had seen her "visitor" about the same time he had seen his. Furthermore, many years later the space people had been kind enough to give her a vision and tell her a little about themselves.

They are spiritual beings, it seems, who have come here from a place called Gilanea. They serve as protectors of the universe. One of their most important functions on earth is to work with many of our planet's children through a process called "mind coding." These children will grow up to be great leaders. They will have a strong belief in the things they are doing, "with a full knowledge of why they are performing their particular missions. There will be great changes among the many cultures that inhabit the Earth."[4]

This concept of "children of God" seems to be a reinterpretation of Bible passages such as 1 John 3:1, 2, which I've already mentioned. And there are others:

> The Spirit himself testifies with our spirit that we are God's children.   Romans 8:16

---

4. Steiger, *The UFO Abductors*, 150.

> Because you are sons, God sent the Spirit of his son into our hearts, the Spirit who calls out, "Abba, Father." So you are no longer a slave but a son; and since you are a son, God has made you also an heir.
> Galatians 4:6

> Therefore come out from them and be separate, says the Lord. Touch no unclean thing, and I will receive you. I will be a Father to you, and you will be my sons and daughters, says the Lord Almighty.
> 2 Corinthians 6:17, 18

How do we become a child of God? The Bible says it happens when we accept the sacrifice God provided for us through the life, death, and resurrection of His Son, Jesus Christ. The visitors say it happens through "mind coding" and "crossbreeding."

Finally, the space people had some very good words for Sharon Reed herself because "Your search for a Superior Being that the churches call God seemed never to end, but then you finally found it—that knowledge of God within your self. You dared to be different, because you had an inner knowledge that told you that you were correct."[5]

The Gilaneans are happy with us, it seems, when we disregard the teachings of the Christian church, discard the words of the Bible, and look to the God within ourselves.

Who are you going to believe? The Gilaneans or the Word of God, which declares:

---

5. Steiger, *The UFO Abductors*, 151.

> If we or an angel from heaven should preach a gospel other than the one we preached to you, let him be eternally condemned! As we have already said, so now I say again: If anybody is preaching to you a gospel other than what you accepted, let him be eternally condemned!   Galatians 1:8, 9

It's interesting how often the visitors refer to God, or the Bible. They have reverence for it because it is a "Holy Book," but when it comes right down to it, they don't want us to believe a single word of it!

In his book *Guardians of the Universe?* Ronald Story states, "It can be said, with certainty, that a psychological 'conditioning process' is taking place, which is either directly or indirectly related to the UFO phenomenon."[6]

The visitors tell us they have come to protect us and serve us. But it seems more likely that they have come to get us to change the way we think about God. Why would they be interested in doing that? Perhaps it is because they are involved in the universal struggle between good and evil that is still being fought in our universe.

The visitors seem to insist on ridding us of the idea that evil exists anywhere except on earth, where it is the result of the general depravity of the human race. Christians agree with that assessment of man's nature. The Bible itself teaches that we have fallen from grace,

---

6. Ronald Story, *Guardians of the Universe?* (New York: St. Martin's Press, 1980), 150.

are all sinners, and therefore that we all need God's grace and mercy.

But the visitors tell us that of all the planets and of all the many types of beings throughout the universe and beyond, only earth has been touched by evil. We are the black sheep of the universe, perhaps because we are not far removed from the beasts, our ancestors. Everywhere else in the cosmos all is goodness and peace and light. There is no devil lurking out there anywhere. Whatever supernatural power exists is wise and good and beneficial.

But that's not what the Bible says. And their proclamations don't square with human experience either.

In the early 1970s at the University of Indiana, a student named Bill Fogarty belonged to an informal group that met once a week to discuss politics, philosophy, and what-have-you. Eventually, members of the group developed an interest in UFOs and visitors from space. The five students in the group were physically fit, nondrinkers, nondopers, and two were Vietnam combat veterans. They were not prone to visions or hallucinations, and yet, soon after the attention of the group turned to flying saucers, the students began to see strange things in the sky and experience other weird goings-on.

Soon the group turned its attention exclusively to UFOs, and the young men got together every evening to search the skies for alien spacecraft. They were not disappointed.

According to Fogarty, they "all witnessed UFOs

cavorting in the midnight sky. On one occasion I stood within ten feet of two nocturnal lights hovering silently in midair. Later we heard rappings in the dark, hollow voices, heavy breathing and the crushing footsteps of unseen entities."

None of the students was overly excited or hysterical about what they witnessed. Instead, they felt pride that they had been singled out for such experiences. They were sure they "could deal rationally with such phenomena and stay in control of the situation."

They were wrong. They couldn't. Suddenly, the experiences became more violent. One of the young men was terrorized in his home by furious pounding on the walls and loud rattling of bedposts. The young man himself was struck hard in the face.

Soon thereafter, members of the group began to sense they were being followed. "Unmarked" cars seemed to tail the young men wherever they went. Some reported that they had awakened in the middle of the night to find strange "dark clad" men standing in their apartments.

Radios and television sets switched on when nobody was close to them, and locked doors sprang open, even though they were still securely locked.

One of the men told his friends that he had suddenly been teleported from his bedroom to the middle of a wooded area on the outskirts of the city. Because the other members of the group had had so many strange things happen to them, they didn't doubt their friend's account.

Fogarty began sleeping with the light on and a gun underneath his pillow.

One of Forgarty's friends "invested heavily in weapons and began running with a group that offered sacrifices to Odin. A third was 'born again' into fundamental Christianity. The other two dropped out of college a month before they would have graduated with honors."[7]

The young men had stumbled into something frightening and uncontrollable. They looked for escape in various ways—two by running away, one by getting deeply involved in the occult, and one by turning to the God of the Bible.

Who were the men who showed up, uninvited, in the middle of someone's apartment during the middle of the night? What was the purpose of their intrusion?

Do the visitors really want to help us? If so, why go about it by frightening people half to death? It is a strange way to bring "enlightenment."

In the years following the strange occurrences, Fogarty spent a great deal of time thinking about what happened to him and his friends. He finally concluded that they had tapped into some sort of "energy" that has always been present on the earth. There wasn't anything "alien" or particularly sinister about it. It was just a force—like the one George Lucas got so much mileage out of in his *Star Wars* trilogy.

But there is a major flaw in that assessment of the

---

7. Steiger, *The UFO Abductors*, 30–32.

A MESSAGE FROM SPACE

situation. A nonpersonal energy doesn't take on human form and invade people's apartments in the middle of the night. Neither does it drive an unmarked car—or any kind of car for that matter.

Many passages in the Bible warn about the dangers of getting involved in the occult. Even though there is nothing immediately apparent to link UFOs to the occult, the bridge is there. Those who become deeply interested in UFOs almost always wind up interested in the occult. Not only interested, in fact, but deeply involved.

[margin note: this doesn't show that they're necessarily linked]

Suppose we were able to send astronauts to some distant planet and they were to discover intelligent life on that planet. Would we make our presence known to them by playing weird tricks on them and sneaking into their homes?

Of course not. We would determine what the proper channels were and, in as nonthreatening a way as possible, announce that we had come for a visit.

If our astronauts went instead to the citizens of that world on a one-to-one basis and recruited individuals to welcome and support them in their mission, the lawful government (and the rest of the citizens of that planet) would have good reason to wonder about us and worry about what we were up to.

That, it seems, is what's happening here on earth. Recruits are being sought one at a time, sometimes in totally unorthodox ways, but successfully just the same.

Jesus said, "I tell you the truth, the man who does not enter the sheep pen by the gate, but climbs in by some other way, is a thief and a robber. The man who enters by the gate is the shepherd of the sheep" (John 10:1, 2).

Jesus may have been talking about sheep and shepherds, but the principle is the same no matter who you're talking about. The true shepherd goes through the main gate instead of climbing over the fence. The real homeowner walks through the front door instead of climbing through the window. And the man who wants to tell us the truth—even if he comes from outer space—broadcasts it openly instead of whispering it into the ears of helpless captives in the middle of the night.

Chapter Four

SAME OLD BOOK WITH A DIFFERENT COVER

OCTOBER 14, 1978, 10:20 P.M.

While driving down a residential street in Denver, Colorado, with her young granddaughter, Jenifer, sound asleep in the seat beside her, Peggy Otis gazed skyward at what she thought was an airplane. A huge airplane, getting lower and lower. No. It was too low! What was going on? It was going to crash into the street!

"Sparks were being emitted from underneath it, and it suddenly came down so low that I thought it was going to smash the top of my car. I screamed at Jenifer to wake up, and jumped out of the car. The craft was dome-shaped, and I could see someone moving inside it. We were terrified thinking that it was going to crush

SAME OLD BOOK WITH A DIFFERENT COVER

us. Then I telepathically received the message, 'Don't forget us,' and it floated away."[1]

Once the craft was gone, Peggy and Jenifer got back into the car, and Peggy drove home as quickly as she could. Her husband called the airport to see if anyone had reported unusual aircraft in the area. No one had. The strange ship emitted a noise like a garbage disposal and came low enough that she could see inside it, but somehow no one else had noticed it.

To help her deal with what had happened, Otis sought a hypnotist. Under hypnosis, she described the man in the aircraft as having a white head, no ears, and slanted eyes. He wasn't more than four feet tall, and he had his hands on "something like a steering wheel."

She felt as if this strange being was drawing her toward him, trying to tell her that he loved her, not to be afraid, and that "they" would be back.

As is so often the case following an experience with a UFO, Peggy Otis soon became interested in the occult. She began "receiving messages" that she and her husband should leave Denver because the climate was unhealthy. Eventually they moved to California, where she began conducting weekly classes in which she and her friends attempted "to raise the vibrations of the world."[2]

The account of Peggy Otis's encounter with an air-

---

1. Ruth Montgomery, *Aliens Among Us* (New York: G. P. Putnam and Sons, 1985), 44.
2. Montgomery, *Aliens Among Us*, 46.

SAME OLD BOOK WITH A DIFFERENT COVER

ship is one of many similar stories from Ruth Montgomery's book *Aliens Among Us*, in which she explains that the worlds of the psychic and the spaceman are intertwined.

At one time, Ruth Montgomery was interested in more down-to-earth matters. From her headquarters in Washington she wrote a syndicated newspaper column dealing with politics and world affairs. Then, in the mid-sixties, she became more interested in out-of-this-world affairs.

Montgomery had become friends with Jeane Dixon, the hottest thing in the psychic world at the time. Dixon had a growing reputation as the world's most gifted psychic. She was a hybrid of occultic practices and Christianity, conjuring up visions in a crystal ball and preaching the reliability of astrology, but making clear that her talent was a gift from God and that she believed in Jesus Christ. (Although she was never clear as to what it was she believed about Jesus.)

Dixon supposedly had read Montgomery's book about Lady Bird Johnson and decided she needed the same writer to help her reach the masses with her story. She apparently found a true believer in Montgomery, who agreed to write her biography.

So the two teamed up to write *A Gift of Prophecy*, which rose quickly to the best-seller lists and stayed there for several weeks. The million-selling book did what Dixon had hoped it would do. It established her as an international celebrity by reporting incident after incident where her powers of precognition had pre-

SAME OLD BOOK WITH A DIFFERENT COVER

vented calamities, saved lives, and generally helped people become better off than they had been.

Although Dixon's book had story after story of things she had correctly predicted in the past, she didn't do as well when it came to predicting the future. In fact, she failed miserably. For example, she predicted that Robert Kennedy would become a great leader who would serve his country well. A few years later he was assassinated. She said that Fidel Castro would soon be removed from power. More than twenty-five years later, he still controls Cuba.

On and on she went, making predictions that looked like pretty good bets in 1965, but which, to put it kindly, simply did not come true.

In the mid-seventies, a newspaper asked me to review a copy of *A Gift of Prophecy* from the perspective of ten years later. I had read the book when it first came out, but couldn't remember much about it. I didn't expect that Jeane Dixon had batted 1.000, but I was astounded to see how often she was obviously and totally wrong. She hadn't even batted .100, and it wasn't as if she was taking big chances with her predictions. Most were simply "sure bets" that hadn't panned out as expected.

Anyone who rechecked her old predictions would have a difficult time believing anything new she had to say. Yet Jeane Dixon continued to be a big name in the psychic world.

Of course Dixon was never shy about changing her mind, so that got her out of some tight spots.

For a while, she was terribly excited about a baby born in the Middle East on February 5, 1962. This remarkable young child was endowed with wisdom and love. Someday he would bring the warring nations of the world together. All nations would pledge allegiance to him and serve under his banner of love.

Later, she changed her mind and said the same child was the antichrist. She hadn't realized this when the visions first came to her, but it became clear that this man would only pretend to represent goodness and light as he worked for his real master—Satan.

Perhaps I'm being cynical, but I wonder if Mrs. Dixon changed her mind because demonism was a hot subject in the 1970s, when *The Exorcist* was a top box-office draw. Or was she seeking to endear herself to Christians looking for the antichrist? Whatever her reasoning, both predictions were wrong. It has been nearly thirty years since she announced the birth of this wonder child, and he still has not shown up on the world scene.

Working with Jeane Dixon was the beginning of Montgomery's total immersion in the occult. When the two of them started working together, Ruth Montgomery was a political writer with a curiosity about supernatural things. By the time they were finished, she exhibited a deep faith in the supernatural and her interest in politics seemed to disappear.

Jeane Dixon is still writing her syndicated horoscopes and giving her once-a-year predictions to tabloids like *The National Enquirer*, but Ruth Montgomery

SAME OLD BOOK WITH A DIFFERENT COVER

has become an even bigger name in occultic circles. She has turned out book after book on psychic matters—spreading the gospel of reincarnation, giving "eyewitness" accounts of what life is like on "the other side," and explaining how our dreams speak to us. Montgomery has acquired her very own "guides" and has become adept at automatic writing, in which she lets her fingers rest on the keys of her typewriter and allows beings from the spirit world to write through her.

Although Montgomery was a tough and skeptical journalist when she started writing about the occult, her recent books have a wide-eyed quality to them. She seems to believe that we live in a wonderful world in a wonderful universe and if we could only throw off our doubts, fears, and general negativity, all would be peace and love and light forever. There is no room for evil in her cosmos, except on the part of poor, misguided earthlings.

The occult world is an exciting and expanding place. There's always room for a new experience or two, a new type of being or two. Disembodied spirits have always lived there, of course, along with assorted other ghosts and goblins. But in the 1980s, space beings moved in.

According to Montgomery, they have come here in ever-increasing numbers. Some are quite content to zip through our atmosphere in their spaceships, even though they are of such a spiritually advanced nature that they don't need mechanical devices for traveling through space. Others have entered human bodies—

SAME OLD BOOK WITH A DIFFERENT COVER

some in a benign form of possession, and others through birth. But whoever they are, and whichever planet they have come from (the visitors claim to come from a number of different ones), Montgomery believes they are all here to help us.

We are especially in need of their presence because earth is about to undergo a tremendous cataclysm in which millions—perhaps billions—of us will be killed. It has nothing to do with nuclear war, toxic waste, new diseases, famine, or anything of the sort. Montgomery's guides have told her that the earth is going to shift on its axis right around the turn of the century, and when that happens, watch out; things will not be the same here for thousands and thousands of years.

Exactly what will happen when this shift occurs? First, oceans will cover some existing land masses, as happened to Atlantis and Lemuria several thousand years ago. There will be earthquakes far beyond anything we've seen in our lifetime, and volcanic eruptions will make Mount St. Helen's look like a tiny firecracker.

As our planet flips on its side, the entire surface of the earth will be rearranged. The poles and the equator will shift. Land that was tropical will be covered with ice, and polar bears and penguins—if any survive—will find themselves in temperatures more suited to parrots and flamingoes.

Most of us know that mammoth carcasses have been found encased in blocks of ice near the North Pole, so well-preserved that it appears they were flash frozen. Scientists have speculated as to how the huge, prehistoric mammals got trapped in ice so far north. It's also been reported that tropical leaves were found in the mouth of one such mammoth. The half-chewed leaves added to the mystery of the mammoth's fate. How did tropical plants get to the Arctic Circle? It's as if one moment the big beast was enjoying an afternoon snack on a balmy afternoon, and the next he was prepared for use by some giant to play the ole "mammoth-in-an-ice-cube" trick on one of his friends.

Thanks to knowledge from her guides, Montgomery knows exactly what happened to that hapless prehistoric fellow. The world shifted on its axis, and that was all she wrote for him and most of his breed.

Take a good look at that guy, she'll tell you, and you'll get a good idea of what's going to happen to us. (Which means that even on the balmiest spring day, it might be a good idea to keep an overcoat handy.)

Montgomery is not the only person receiving messages of impending doom. Thelma Terrell, better known to her followers as Tuella (the name given to her by her space friends who apparently want her to have a more cosmic-sounding name than Thelma), has published several booklets that contain messages given to her by Commander Ashtar, who is in charge of an intergalactic fleet of spaceships that have been orbiting our planet for several hundred years.

Ashtar, speaking through Tuella, wants us to know that most of the earth's residents will lose their physical lives when the planet shifts on its axis. A number of "enlightened" ones, however, will be evacuated by his forces so the planet can repopulate once everything has calmed down again.

Andromeda Rex, another space person who supposedly speaks through Tuella, told her, "Our rescue ships will be able to come in close enough in the twinkling of an eye to set the lifting beams in operation in a moment. Mankind will be lifted, levitated shall we say, by the beams from our smaller ships."[3]

If all this sounds to you like unimaginative science fiction, you're not alone. Montgomery admits that even she found Tuella's pronouncements hard to believe—until her guides assured her it is all true.

Tuella, like an Old Testament prophet entrusted with spreading the Word of God, is doing her best to get us to listen.

Montgomery writes:

> I protested that I was somewhat turned off by some of her messages that purport to come from Jesus, the Mother Mary and other saints, and the Guides responded: "She would be wise not to infuse so much Biblical religion into her messages, as the Ashtar Command is nondenominational and like all spacelings worships the one Creator of us all. She is not actually hearing from the ones you mention, but is feeling what they might have conveyed. We don't like to see the issue unduly tied in with Biblical stories, for the worldwide appearance of space people is not solely limited to those

---

3. Montgomery, *Aliens Among Us*, 51, 52.

spiritual beings who have trod the earth, but includes ones from other areas of space and other galaxies."[4]

Montgomery, upon the authority of her "guides," is willing to accept that Tuella is hearing from space beings with names like Ashtar, Andromeda Rex, Lord Kuthumi, and Monka, but the minute the name of Jesus is mentioned she wants to chuck the whole thing out the window.

Again it becomes obvious that we cannot have it both ways. If Jesus Christ is who He said He was, the only begotten Son of the Creator of us all, these space beings are not who they claim to be. Otherwise they would acknowledge the Lordship of Christ.

Montgomery is hearing from someone. Tuella is apparently hearing from someone. And if neither is hearing from spiritual beings of goodness and light, just who are they hearing from?

When Montgomery continued to question her guides about the messages from Commander Ashtar, she was told that these communications come to those who practice meditation and who are open to them. In other words, if you allow your mind to become as quiet as possible, if you empty it of all thought and reach out to the spacemen, they will answer.

And it's probably true. There are voices whispering in the wind. There are beings who would like nothing better than for us to be open to their message. But be-

---

4. Montgomery, *Aliens Among Us*, 52, 53.

SAME OLD BOOK WITH A DIFFERENT COVER

cause they rarely tell the truth about anything, it's extremely unlikely that we're really hearing from Commander Ashtar, Andromeda Rex, or any of the Space Brothers.

UFO investigator Jacques Vallee, the role model for LaCombe in the movie *Close Encounters of the Third Kind*, met a woman named Helen who had encountered a UFO. Vallee checked out her story from every angle and was convinced that she was telling the truth.

After her encounter, Helen became obsessed with building a type of motor, the instructions for which were given to her by the UFOnauts. Nothing mattered to her except building a working model of that motor, and thus revolutionizing earth's technology.

There was only one problem. The motor cannot work. It is based on a "perpetual motion" theory that has been put forth many times throughout the years, usually by some con artist trying to get a hefty investment for his invention.

Howard Menger, another contactee, devoted much of his time and energy developing a "free-energy motor" designed by beings from space. But once again, the invention that would revolutionize life on earth was absolutely worthless.

Are these "guardians of our planet" cruel practical jokers instead? Did they titter and slap their hands over their mouths when they watched Peggy Otis and her friends attempting to "raise the vibrations of the world?" Were they laughing up their sleeves as they watched Helen spend every waking hour trying to build a motor that never had the slightest chance of working? Did they break into guffaws when Howard Menger went on television to explain how his "free-energy motor" would work? Are they beside themselves with hysterical laughter when they give Tuella another one of their lengthy messages and ask her to get it published so we can all be warned of the earth's impending doom?

In *Transformation*, Whitley Strieber tells of how terrified he was when his visitors told him he was going to die on an upcoming airplane trip. When the day of the trip came, Strieber wanted to cancel, but didn't. If this was to be his fate, there was nothing he could do about it anyway. Getting on board was one of the most difficult things he ever did. He was overcome with sadness as he thought about his wife and son going through life without him. He also was afraid of dying, even though his visitors had taught him that life goes on beyond the grave, going so far as to tell him they were here "to recycle souls."[5]

At first, the trip was uneventful. But then it happened. Thunder, lightning, and turbulent winds tossed the airplane violently. Despite the pilot's announcements that everything would be all right, Strieber knew otherwise. He was going to die and so, probably, were all of the other people on board.

But suddenly Strieber realized it didn't matter. Dying wasn't going to be so bad. Immediately, all his fear vanished, and he was completely at peace. He had

---

5. Strieber, *Transformation*, 198.

confronted his deepest fear; and through confronting it, he had conquered it.

When the airplane landed safely and Strieber walked away without a scratch, he decided that this was what the visitors had been talking about. When they told him he was going to die, they meant that he would come face-to-face with his worst fears and, in facing them, be resurrected into a new way of living.

Despite all Strieber says about it, the fact remains that the visitors told him, quite plainly, that he would be killed on that airplane ride. The truth is that his "friends" put him through several hours of unnecessary pain and terror. He says they did it to make a better person out of him. Maybe they did it for laughs.

In the 1950s, many UFO contactees were told that the truth about flying saucers would be released within a few years. It didn't happen.

The Two promised to take their followers with them to a faraway paradise. That didn't happen either.

Helen and Howard spent countless hours working on motors that space beings said would revolutionize the earth's technology. Both were worthless.

Whitley Strieber was told that he would be killed in an airplane crash. He wasn't.

I have no idea how a mammoth happened to be flash frozen at the North Pole, nor how he got tropical leaves in his mouth. Perhaps the earth slipped on its axis thousands of years ago; perhaps some other cataclysmic event caused it, or perhaps there is a simpler, gentler answer.

SAME OLD BOOK WITH A DIFFERENT COVER

Even if the earth did slip on its axis once, that doesn't mean it's going to happen again. And if the track record of "space beings" and "spirit guides" is any indication, it's not about to happen any time soon.

If it doesn't happen when predicted, true believers will simply push the events twenty-five or thirty years into the future. In the year 2010, we'll probably be hearing that the mystery of the UFOs is about to be solved.

LEGACY OF THE BELIEVERS

In the California desert, near the community of Yucca Valley, stands a huge metallic structure that was built by George Van Tassel at the bidding of his friends from outer space. Built entirely without nails or other metallic fasteners, the structure is called the "Integratron," and it is specifically designed to reverse the aging process.

Van Tassel, an intelligent but ordinary man who had an aptitude for science, had been an aircraft mechanic for Douglas, Hughes, and Lockheed. He worked a regular job and lived a regular life until an encounter with "The Council of Seven Lights" changed him completely. He quit his job, moved to the high desert country of Southern California, and built his unusual edifice. He also founded a group called the Ministry of Universal Wisdom and devoted the rest of his life to spreading the message of universal brotherhood.

Van Tassel claimed that the "Integratron" used principles of "electrostatic generation" to change the cell structure of the human body, and thus slow down the aging process. Thousands of people were attracted to Van Tassel's teachings. Between 1954 and 1970 many of them came to Yucca Valley every year for a UFO convention.

Unfortunately, Van Tassel himself apparently didn't spend enough time inside the "Integratron." He died in 1978 at the age of sixty-eight—another case of a promise from the "Space Brothers" remaining unfulfilled.

In the 1960s, a group called the "Light Affiliates" was organized in British Columbia. The members of the group got their instructions from a space being who said his name was Ox-Ho. Ox-Ho gave the Light Affiliates several minor prophecies, all of which were fulfilled right on schedule. Then, having won their confidence, he dropped the bombshell. Judgment Day for the earth was due to arrive on November 22, 1969.

Armed with this knowledge, members of the organization set about the task of getting their affairs in order and preparing for the end of the world. But November 22 came and went without the slightest cosmic disturbance, and Mr. Ox-Ho apparently sped away into the dark reaches of the universe, laughing up his sleeve all the while.

George Adamski, a contemporary of George Van Tassel's, also ran into beings from space on the California desert. Adamski's best space friends were from Venus, although he met beings from many other planets as well. He was assured, in fact, that every planet in our solar system had life on it, and that the moon was a very busy way station for interplanetary travelers. The earth was like a poor, backward wilderness, truly a third-world planet when compared with the wonders elsewhere in the solar system.

Years after Adamski's death, and years after a succession of unmanned spacecraft have surveyed every planet of the universe and found one desolate and lifeless landscape after another, some still believe in him.

Jacques Bordas, a contactee in France, has been told that he will not grow older and that his mind will open itself to receive universal truths. Those who have contacted him claim to be from Titan, one of the moons of Saturn, although Bordas admits that he doesn't know whether this is true or whether they told him that simply because it's something he can understand.

In a conversation with UFO investigator Jacques Vallee, he said, "They could well be saying this because it is something I can understand. I have no proof that it's true. Besides, there are Luciferian forces out there...."

When asked to elaborate on what he meant by Luciferian forces, and whether he was referring to a battle of good and evil, he said, "No, I do not mean that. Those are simply forces of a different type, which we are not able to comprehend. When we have evolved sufficiently, we will realize that the contradiction was only an apparent one."[6]

---

6. Jacques Vallee, *Messengers of Deception* (Berkeley, Calif.: And/Or Press, 1979), 85.

In other words, "When is a lie not a lie?" When it is told by someone who claims to be from outer space.

In the 1950s, when earthlings were beginning to take their first shaky steps into space and when we were still speculating about what we'd find on the moon and the planets beyond, the creatures who came to us claimed to be from Mars, Venus, or Neptune. But as our explorers pushed farther into space and found nothing but silence and desolate waste, the aliens claimed to be from farther away.

Now some say they are from Titan, a world scientists tell us might have an atmosphere similar to that of the earth, even though it's many millions of miles farther from the sun and therefore, presumably, bitterly cold. Or they tell us they are from Zeta Reticuli, Sirius, or other more esoteric stars, such as Wolf 24. Others give names that seem to be made up, or which don't have any connection to reality as we know it. Remember Lanulos and Gilanea?

VOICES FROM OUIJA BOARDS— AND ELSEWHERE

Not too long after my wife and I were married, my father passed away. I was only twenty years old and had a hard time dealing with the loss. Although my father had been a minister and I had been raised with the traditional Christian understanding of salvation and the afterlife, I needed some extra reassurance that my father was indeed alive and well, somewhere out there.

I began to read everything I could find on the subject of immortality, without bothering to consider the source.

Eventually I purchased a Ouija board to see if I could contact my father, or, for that matter, anyone else on "the other side" who had attained wisdom. (It didn't occur to me until later that death doesn't necessarily give anyone the key to the secrets of the universe.)

My wife, Diane, and I found that the Ouija board responded immediately to our touch. All we had to do was lightly put our fingers on the planchette, and it began to fly all over the board, giving us advice and answers to our deepest questions.

My father was an educated man, but he was a notoriously poor speller. He always had my mother look over anything he wrote to doublecheck the spelling.

I quickly made contact with an entity who, although he (it?) would not tell me who he was, had a bit of difficulty with spelling. On one occasion, we asked if he would tell us his name.

"No," came the reply.

"Why not?"

"Becaus," came the answer, "he is dead."

In other words, because the entity had "passed over" he was no longer who he had been during his earthly life. But that *e* left off the end of *Because* was almost enough to convince me that I had established contact with my father.

On another occasion, I asked the board to name the planet nearest to the earth with life on it.

The planchette began to move: "Z–Y–G–L–O–S."

I looked across at Diane and said, "Well, obviously it's spelling the name of a planet we've never heard of."

Although the statement wasn't addressed to the Ouija board, or to the entity operating it, the planchette immediately shot up to "Yes."

Through events I won't relate here, I became convinced that I was not in contact with my father at all, nor do I believe there is a planet named Zyglos that is populated.

My point is, whatever we know, whatever we learn, the "Space Brothers" are always just slightly out of our grasp. They are like mirages we see ahead of us as we drive down a long stretch of highway on a hot summer day. No matter how fast or how far we go, we can never reach them.

What's more, the aliens seem to be one step beyond our reach in terms of their technology as well as in where they live.

In 1211, people in a tiny Irish village were disturbed one Sunday afternoon to see a strange cigar-shaped aircraft come floating over their town. They were even more disturbed when the craft came close to the ground and an anchor was tossed out. Following that, a ladder was lowered, and a strange little man in a metallic suit climbed down. After looking around for a few minutes, he climbed back up the ladder into the craft, which quickly ascended into the afternoon sky.[7]

---

7. Robert Emenegger, *UFOs Past, Present & Future* (New York: Ballantine Books, 1975), 5.

SAME OLD BOOK WITH A DIFFERENT COVER

In today's frame of reference, a new movie would be laughed out of the theatre if it depicted the landing of an interplanetary spacecraft as descending slowly out of the clouds, and then, when it is fifteen feet or so above the ground, a door opens and a cast-iron anchor is tossed out to keep the craft from drifting away.

Our technology has advanced far enough that the thought of an anchor being tossed out of an aircraft, and especially an aircraft capable of traveling millions of miles through space, is ludicrous. But in the thirteenth century it seemed futuristic, not antiquated.

In the early 1800s, slow-moving, cigar-shaped craft were sometimes reported in European skies—years before dirigibles were first built, but not that many years before.

Good question

It makes you wonder, doesn't it? If these creatures are so far advanced, why is their technology just one small jump ahead of us? Why are they advanced only to the point we can understand? Or could it be that these beings are really only a reflection of our own dreams and imaginations?

A few years ago, I was privileged to meet Ben Alexander, a tall, distinguished-looking gentleman who heads an organization called Exposing Satan's Power. Alexander is not some nut who sees Satan and his angels of darkness lurking in every shadow. But he has a very good reason for doing what he does.

For several years, in his native England, Alexander was a spirit medium, and a good one. Not only did voices speak through him, but a substance called ectoplasm poured out of his body and took the shape of entities from "the other side."

Alexander believed totally in what he was doing and enjoyed being able to help people by putting them in contact with their dead loved ones. He convinced even the most hardened skeptics by the messages he was able to bring from those "dear departed" souls. Time after time he would hear comments such as, "This has to be Joe; nobody knew that but him and me!"

Alexander considered himself a Christian. He attended a spiritualist church, which kept paintings of Jesus Christ on the walls and which would often combine the Lord's Supper with a seance. The church taught that Jesus Christ had been the greatest spirit medium who had ever lived.

But Alexander had an increasingly hard time reconciling the teachings of his church with what the Bible said. Specifically, he had a very difficult time explaining away Deuteronomy 18:9–12:

> When you enter the land the Lord your God is giving you, do not learn to imitate the detestable ways of the nations there. Let no one be found among you who sacrifices his son or daughter in the fire, who practices divination or sorcery, interprets omens, engages in witchcraft, or casts spells, or who is a medium or spiritist or who consults the dead. Anyone who does these things is detestable to the Lord.

He found it impossible to reconcile that clear warning against consulting the dead with his church's teaching that Jesus Christ was nothing more than a glorified medium.

Eventually, Alexander became convinced that he was not really in touch with the departed friends and loved ones of the people who paid for his services. He was in touch with someone who knew all the deepest and darkest secrets of everyone who came to him, but it wasn't someone with a very pleasant personality.

When Alexander began to think seriously about giving up spiritualism and surrendering his life to Christ, the entities that he had been in touch with became increasingly violent. On one occasion, a Bible he was reading was snatched out of his hands and thrown across the room. Pages were torn out of it. Threatening messages were left for him saying "they" would be waiting for him on the other side.

Nevertheless, Alexander denounced his involvement in spiritualism and today spends as much time as possible warning against its dangers.

What does this have to do with UFOs and creatures from space? Plenty.

Remember Al Bender. He discovered that these beings from space are responsible for all of the psychic phenomena taking place on the earth today.

Ruth Montgomery says the same thing, although she fuzzes the lines so much that it's hard to tell where "brothers from space" leave off and "spirits of the dead" begin. As far as she is concerned, these beings from space have a better understanding of life and death than

SAME OLD BOOK WITH A DIFFERENT COVER

those of us who are earth-bound. They know all about reincarnation, and they seem to operate most comfortably in some sort of fourth dimension where the souls of deceased earthlings are also found in abundance.

Could these voices, which claim to come from the other side of the grave, originate with beings from outer space? Or is it possible that the voices claiming to come from outer space really come from disembodied spirits? Perhaps they say they are from space so we'll be more inclined to listen to them. Or is there a third solution? Could these voices have another point of origin—and could the truth be far more sinister than we've dreamed?

In his book *UFOs: Operation Trojan Horse*, prominent UFO investigator John Keel writes:

> Thousands of mediums, psychics and UFO contactees have been receiving mountains of messages from "Ashtar" in recent years. Mr. Ashtar represents himself as a leader in the great intergalactic councils which hold regular meetings on Jupiter, Venus, Saturn and many planets known to us. But Ashtar is not a new arrival. Variations of this name, such as Astaroth, Ashar, Asharoth, etc., appear in demonological literature throughout history, both in the Orient and the Occident. Mr. Ashtar had been around a very long time, posing as assorted gods and demons and now, in the modern phase, as another glorious spaceman.[8]

---

8. John A. Keel, *UFOs: Operation Trojan Horse* (New York: G. P. Putnam & Sons, 1970), 230.

Ashtar, or one of his cousins, was one of the pagan gods the Israelites were commanded not to worship when they came into the Promised Land.[9] When they came into Canaan they were to "Break down their altars, smash their sacred stones and burn their Asherah poles in the fire; cut down the idols of their gods and wipe out their names from those places" (Deuteronomy 12:3).

Who is this Ashtar? A spaceman piloting his spacecraft through the farthest reaches of the universe? Or a demon bent on deceiving as many of us as he possibly can? Or nothing more than a shadowy creature born of overactive imaginations?

THE GHOST WHO NEVER EXISTED

In 1972, several members of the Toronto Society for Psychical Research got together to create their own ghost. The idea was to create a phantom and then get it to manifest itself to them.

According to published reports, they succeeded beyond their wildest dreams.[10]

The group named their ghost Philip. After deciding he had lived in seventeenth-century England, they commissioned a member of the group, a writer, to write the account of Philip's life, making it as romantic and heroic as possible. Another member, an artist, was asked

---

9. Asherah is another name for Ashteroth or Ashtar. And Ishtar was the premier goddess of ancient Babylonia and Assyria.
10. Lynn Picknett, *Flights of Fancy* (New York: Ballantine Books, 1987), 173–176.

SAME OLD BOOK WITH A DIFFERENT COVER

to paint a portrait of this man who never existed. The other members of the group were asked to learn everything they could about Philip, and to do their best to believe in him. Following that, they would attempt to contact him "on the other side."

The group members sat around a table. Resting their hands lightly on the surface, they asked Philip to please make his presence known to them.

During succeeding weeks, they made several attempts to contact Philip. Months went by without the slightest response, but the members wouldn't give up. Finally they were rewarded when their creation decided to put in an appearance. They were seated around the table calling out, "Hello, Philip," when a series of sharp raps sounded.

As time went by, Philip became more extroverted and quickly made his presence known every time the research group got together. When they asked him questions, he would reply by loudly rapping out his answers on the table's surface.

His answers to questions about his life always corroborated what had been written about him, although in some instances he reportedly added details of his own.

The members of the group often sang to Philip, at which time he (or the table, at least) would join in by bouncing up and down in time with the music.

Group members also reported that the table would playfully chase them around the room, and on one occasion it became wedged in the doorway after trying to follow one of the researchers out of the room.

SAME OLD BOOK WITH A DIFFERENT COVER

Finally the time came to introduce Philip to the world. And so they took the table to the studios of Toronto City Television, where a show on paranormal activity was being taped in front of a live audience.

Philip was not bothered in the least by stage fright. When the show's moderator called out, "Hello, Philip," he responded with the usual loud raps—and then the table was off on an inspection tour, walking around the studio, bumping and bouncing along like something out of *Fantasia*.

For the next several minutes, the moderator, panel members, and the studio audience asked Philip questions. He answered all of them in the usual way. He was surely one of the most extroverted "ghosts" in all of history. Even though he had never really existed at all.

The only thing Philip couldn't abide was a lack of faith. At one point, a member of the Toronto group told him he didn't really exist: "We only made you up, you know."

Upon hearing that, Philip fell silent and could be coaxed to reappear only after members of the group redoubled their efforts to believe in him.

Who was Philip? What was the strange power behind his existence? Was he merely a product of the energy of the human mind? Or was his appearance the result of some demonic masquerade? Had the entity controlling Philip been fooled into thinking the imaginary ghost had been a real person? Did he then seize the opportunity to take over Philip's personality to get his own message across? Are there sinister entities somewhere out there waiting to gain entrance into our hearts and souls through any means possible?

And if so, why? Are we pawns in a cosmic chess game between the forces of light and darkness?

Ben Alexander is convinced that the Bible warns against attempts to contact the dead because God knew we would be opening ourselves up to all sorts of unsavory characters, and that we would wind up being deceived.

The visitors tell us they are here to help us find ourselves in the light of eternity. Whoever we are, whatever we believe, we have already achieved eternal life; all we have to do is reach out and grab it. Life will roll along merrily beyond the grave for all who have ever lived upon this planet.

And yet the Bible says, "For God so loved the world that he gave his one and only Son, that whoever believes in him shall not perish but have eternal life" (John 3:16). And "He who has the Son has life; he who does not have the Son of God does not have life" (1 John 5:12).

Again we are forced to make a choice. We can't have it both ways. We can't believe that Jesus Christ gave His life to save us from our sins and at the same time believe we're all okay and that we never needed His sacrifice in the first place. That's like saying, "Listen, Jesus, we really appreciate what you're trying to do for us, but we really don't need it."

Time and again, the Bible warns us about forces that would like nothing better than to deceive us and take us down the road to destruction. The Apostle Paul said, "Our struggle is not against flesh and blood, but against the rulers, against the authorities, against the powers of this dark world and against the spiritual forces of evil in the heavenly realms" (Ephesians 6:12).

The late Dr. J. Allen Hynek, who served as chairman of the astronomy department of Northwestern University and who was a consultant to Project Blue Book, the United States Air Force's investigation into UFOs, said:

> I have the impression that the UFOs are announcing a change that is coming soon in our scientific paradigms. I am very much afraid that UFOs are related to certain psychic phenomena.
>
> Certainly the phenomenon has psychic aspects. I don't talk about them very much because to a general audience the words "psychic" and "occult" have bad overtones. They say, "Aw, it's all crazy." But the fact is that there are psychic things, for instance, UFOs seem to materialise and dematerialise. There are people who've had UFO experiences who've claimed to have developed psychic ability. There have been reported cases of healings in close encounters and there have been reported cases of precognition, where people had foreknowledge or forewarning that they were going to see something. There has been a change of outlook, a change of philosophy of persons' lives. Now you see, those are rather tricky things to talk about openly, but it's there.

SAME OLD BOOK WITH A DIFFERENT COVER

> Many people... feel that it might be a conditioning process.[11]

How interesting. Somebody wants us to change our views about science, religion, God, and the nature of life beyond the grave. *So are some people; that doesn't make them demons*

Ruth Montgomery believes "our space friends are now ready for us to know that they are here."[12]

Not only ready, in fact, but anxious. It seems unlikely, however, that they are anxious to take off their masks and let us know who they really are.

---

11. Story, *Guardians of the Universe?* 149, 150.
12. Montgomery, *Aliens Among Us*, 75.

CHAPTER FIVE

SO SOMEBODY'S LYING—BUT WHY?

HE'S ONE OF TELEVISION'S FAVORITE PERFORMERS. He makes the commercials more fun than the programs. His name is Joe Isuzu, and he simply cannot tell the truth. He's a sleazy, greasy guy, and he's hysterically funny. At the first sight of him, we know he's going to lie, and sure enough, he always does.

Nobody watches one of his commercials and says, "Well, you know, truth isn't really absolute, so maybe he's not lying after all. Sure, he's made some strange statements, and they sound impossible, but maybe after we've all evolved to a higher plane we'll be able to understand and reconcile his statements with the larger truth."

SO SOMEBODY'S LYING—BUT WHY?

If anybody talked that way, we'd advise him to visit the nearest psychiatrist.

But "the visitors," the "Space Brothers," or whatever we decide to call them, seem disinclined to tell the truth about their origins—or anything else for that matter. Yet thousands of people go on listening to them, hanging on to every word as if it were coming from God Himself.

And that most definitely isn't so.

They have made up one story after another about where they're from, why they're here, and what's going to happen in the future.

Although thousands of people believe every word that purports to come from outer space, I personally would have a difficult time buying a used car from Ashtar and his buddies.

As far as I know, the only reason for lying is to conceal the truth. A person who lies wants to hide something that might be unpleasant—either for you, for him, or for both of you.

Suppose a friend who just bought a sweater at J. C. Penney told you he bought it at Sears.

You'd go off wondering why anyone would lie about something like that. Unless somebody is a psychopathic liar, he won't make up stories about such insignificant things.

But if your friend did something he knew you wouldn't like, he'd be more inclined to lie about it. Suppose, for instance, that you were boycotting J. C. Penney because of a bad experience you had there. If that

SO SOMEBODY'S LYING—BUT WHY?

were the case, he might tell you he bought his sweater at Sears to keep you from getting upset.

People tell lies every day, some more than others. But there's almost always a reason behind the deception.

In the same way, it doesn't make sense to think, "Well, the visitors used to say they came from Venus and now they say they're from Zeta Reticuli—but they're just giving us information that we can understand."

If they really come from Zeta Reticuli, or Wolf 24, or some other star system, why haven't they told their contactees right from the beginning?

Are they lying because they know we wouldn't like it very much if we knew who they really were and where they really came from? And there is an even more important question to ask: Are they lying to us because they are playing a cosmic game of follow-the-leader? Perhaps they want to be like the Pied Piper, leading us who-knows-where, and they know we wouldn't follow them the first step if we knew who they were really working for and where they really want to take us.

Does that sound farfetched or alarmist? Just remember what the Bible says: "For Satan himself masquerades as an angel of light . . . his servants masquerade as servants of righteousness" (2 Corinthians 11:14, 15).

Deception from the heavens is nothing new.

Today Commander Ashtar pours out his New Age bible through servants such as Tuella. One hundred and

SO SOMEBODY'S LYING—BUT WHY?

is this a valid comparison?

sixty years ago, the servant was a young man named Joseph Smith. But the deceivers came to him as angels of light, not as space pilots. In 1830, more people believed in angels than in interplanetary travelers.

Joseph Smith's parents were farmers in upstate New York, near the town of Palmyra. One night while he was seeking guidance for his life, Smith, then twenty-five, was startled when a magnificently built, muscular, and yet very gentle man stood before him.

The visitor told Smith that his name was Moroni and that he had come directly from the presence of God. Smith had been chosen to restore the true Christian church, whose doctrines had been corrupted or lost in the years since the last apostle had died.

There was nothing special about Joseph. He didn't have much in the way of education. He hadn't demonstrated any particular leadership abilities. He wasn't a great orator, and he came from a poor family.

And yet God had chosen him, just as he had chosen David, the least of the sons of Jesse, and Gideon, who said he was the least member in the least important family of all Israel.

There was never a second, apparently, when Joseph Smith doubted the angel's calling on his life.

Moroni told Smith that he was to go to a nearby hillside where he would find some gold and bronze tablets covered with hieroglyphics. He was to translate them into English, even though he knew nothing about hieroglyphics or any other foreign language.

Smith followed Moroni's instructions. He went to

94

SO SOMEBODY'S LYING—BUT WHY?

the exact spot on the hillside that the angel had told him about and began digging. He didn't have to dig very far until he hit something. Sure enough, there they were, just as the angel had said—the miraculous plates that would help him bring God's truths to this latter day. The young man carried them home and began to translate them.

Word spread quickly throughout the small community, and several friends and neighbors of the Smith family later gave written testimony that Joseph Smith was not lying about this, because they had seen him at work translating the plates. Most of them became members of the church Joseph Smith was founding—the Church of Jesus Christ of Latter-day Saints—more commonly known as the Mormon church.

Those plates must have been huge. Either that or the writing on them was incredibly small, because Joseph Smith translated, and translated, and translated some more. For days he was consumed by the task at hand. He wrote like a man possessed—and maybe he was. He wrote until his hand cramped and he developed calluses on his fingers, but still the words kept coming. For days he could not tear himself away from his divinely appointed task, except to eat and sleep—and he did very little of either.

He kept on for hundreds of pages, writing in a style that closely mimicked the English in the King James Version of the Bible. He wrote about how Jesus had come to America. About how the Indians—or Lamanites, as he called them—were the lost tribes of Israel.

He told story after story about godly heroes and their families. He explained about God, the role of Jesus Christ, and the place of man in the universe.

When Smith finally finished his laborious task, the angel Moroni reappeared and announced that he was going to take the tablets back to heaven with him.

The fact that Smith could no longer produce the mysterious tablets increased the skepticism of some of the people who heard what he had done. Where was the proof, they wanted to know, that the tablets had ever existed?

But there was that manuscript, and that was hard to explain away.

If Joseph Smith had been interested in making a name for himself or playing some sort of practical joke, he might have written twenty-five or thirty pages—perhaps even fifty. But why go on for hundreds of pages and hundreds of thousands of words? It just didn't make sense.

And why would so many of the family's acquaintances vouch for Joseph? What benefit could they possibly receive from all this?

Before he was visited by the angel, Joseph Smith had been gaining a reputation around Palmyra as a seer—although not a particularly good one. With the help of certain metals and charms, Smith had been involved in at least one attempt to find a hidden treasure for a client.

In the *Chenango Union* newspaper of Norwich, New York, W. D. Purple, a man who knew Smith, wrote:

SO SOMEBODY'S LYING—BUT WHY?

> In the year 1825, we often saw in that quiet hamlet Joseph Smith, Jr. . . . (living with) the family of Deacon Isaiah Stowell . . . (who had) a monomaniacal impression to seek for hidden treasures, which he believed were hidden in the earth. . . .
>
> Mr. Stowell . . . heard of the fame of . . . Joseph, who by the aid of a magic stone had become a famous seer of lost or hidden treasures. . . . He with the magic stone was at once transferred from his humble abode to the more pretentious mansion of Deacon Stowell.
>
> Here, in the estimation of the Deacon, he confirmed his conceded powers as a seer, by means of the stone which he placed in his hat and by excluding the light from all other terrestrial things could see whatever he wished, even in the depths of the earth.
>
> In February 1826, the sons of Mr. Stowell, who lived with their father, were greatly incensed against Smith, as they plainly saw their father squandering his property in the fruitless search for hidden treasures . . . and caused the arrest of Smith. . . .[1]

Court records reveal that Joseph Smith was found guilty of the crime of fraud.

My point is not to defame the character of Joseph Smith. The court's verdict notwithstanding, it's possible that he seriously attempted to find buried treasure for

---
1. *Chenango* (N.Y.) *Union*, May 3, 1877.

Deacon Stowell, and that he had no intention of defrauding his employer.

My point is that Smith was not, at least in those early days, a particularly pious man who sought to follow God's will in every area of his life. If so, he wouldn't have involved himself in such mystical and magical practices, which are not at all in accordance with the teachings of the Bible.

Joseph Smith had opened himself up to supernatural forces and was eventually "rewarded" with his visit from the angel Moroni.

Joseph Smith had it on "divine authority" that the universe was full of life. In the *Young Woman's Journal* in 1892, Mormon teacher O. B. Huntington wrote:

> As far back as 1837, I knew that he (Joseph Smith) said the moon was inhabited by men and women the same as this earth, and that they lived to a greater age than we do—that they live generally to near the age of 1,000 years.
>
> He described the men as averaging near six feet in height, and dressing quite uniformly in something near the Quaker style.
>
> In my Patriarchal blessing, given by the father of Joseph the Prophet, in Kirtland, 1837, I was told that I should preach the gospel before I was 21 years of age; that I should preach the gospel to the inhabitants upon the islands of the sea, and—to the inhabitants of the moon, even the planet you can now behold with your eyes.

SO SOMEBODY'S LYING—BUT WHY?

The first two promises have been fulfilled, and the latter may be verified.

From the verification of two promises we may resonably expect the third to be fulfilled also.

A strange mixture of Christianity, mythology, and UFOism is found almost every time you dig deeply into UFO lore. This sort of talk didn't originate with Erich Von Daniken and *Chariots of the Gods*. It's been around for at least 160 years.

In Mormon theology, the God who rules the earth is not the God of the entire universe. There are many civilizations in space, and all are under the control of a different god.[2]

As a matter of fact, Mormons believe that everyone living on earth has the potential to be a god. If you are a good Mormon, you may someday rule over your own planet and listen to the prayers and praises of your people.

The teachings of the Mormon church are very much like the teachings given to Ruth Montgomery by her "guides." There may be an allusion to Jesus Christ or God, but neither of these terms is used in the traditional Christian sense.

Her guides may consider Jesus a great teacher. They may say He came to this planet from outer space, or that He was an earthling of immense wisdom and

---

2. Walter R. Martin, *The Kingdom of the Cults* (Minneapolis: Bethany Fellowship, Inc., 1965), 178, 179.

power. But they never present Him as the one and only begotten Son of God, nor do they consider His sacrifice on the cross necessary for us to obtain eternal life.

They tell us we have always been immortal, that we are a part of the brotherhood of the universe. There is no such thing as evil—only "apparent" evil, and one day all these apparent contradictions will be reconciled.

It sounds terrific. But it just doesn't make sense.

ANOTHER "HOLY" BOOK

The Book of Mormon and the other "divinely inspired" writings of Joseph Smith were not the last such works to be given to the world. In 1955, *The Urantia Book* was published. *Urantia*, according to the book's authors and publishers, is the name other residents of the cosmos call planet earth.

Distributed from Chicago by the Urantia Foundation, the book describes the many forms of life that exist throughout the many universes.

The Urantia Foundation says very little about the origin of this book, although it reportedly was dictated by someone who went into a trance to receive messages from the celestial beings who spoke through him.

In a note to new readers of their book, the members of the Urantia Foundation write, "We hope your experience with the Urantia teachings will enhance and deepen your relationship with God and your fellow man, and provide renewed hope, comfort, and reassurance in your daily life."

The Urantia Book dwarfs *The Book of Mormon* in size

and scope. The author (or authors, whichever the case may be) goes on for more than two thousand pages, giving an exhausting, and many times bewildering, description of the various life forms throughout the universe. There is an amazing consistency to the book. Although some parts of it might be considered outright "weird," other parts border on elegance.

There is a long section on the life of Jesus, which sometimes seems to offer even the most sincere Christian new insights into Christ's life.

For example:

> The Jews had heard of a God who would forgive repentant sinners and try to forget their misdeeds, but not until Jesus came, did men hear about a God who went in search of lost sheep, who took the initiative in looking for sinners, and who rejoiced when he found them willing to return to the Father's house. This positive note in religion Jesus extended even to his prayers. And he converted the negative golden rule into a positive admonition of human fairness.[3]

Certainly there are nuggets of truth and insight in those words, and their clarity and flow surpasses anything found in *The Book of Mormon* with its stilted parroting of King James English. But there are also words like these, which attempt to stress the significance of

---

3. *The Urantia Book* (Chicago: The Urantia Foundation, 1955), 1770, 1771.

Jesus' death on the cross, even while discounting the importance of the crucifixion:

> Although Jesus did not die this death on the cross to atone for the racial guilt of mortal man nor to provide some sort of effective approach to an otherwise offended and unforgiving God; even though the Son of Man did not offer himself as a sacrifice to appease the wrath of God and to open the way for sinful man to obtain salvation; notwithstanding that these ideas of atonement and propitiation are erroneous, nonetheless, there are significances attached to the death of Jesus on the cross which should not be overlooked. It is a fact that Urantia has become known among other neighboring planets as the "World of the Cross."[4]

There are also these words, directly denying the sacrificial nature of Christ's death:

> There is no direct relation between the death of Jesus and the Jewish Passover. True, the Master did lay down his life in the flesh on this day, the day of the preparation for the Jewish passover, and at about the time of the sacrificing of the Passover lambs in the temple. But this coincidental occurrence does not in any manner indicate that the death of the Son of Man on earth has any connection with the Jewish sacrificial system. Jesus was a Jew, but as the Son of Man he was a mortal of the realms. The events already narrated and lead-

---

4. *The Urantia Book*, 2016.

ing up to this hour of the Master's impending crucifixion are sufficient to indicate that his death at about this time was a purely natural and man-managed affair.[5]

The Urantia Book denies that Christ's death on the cross served any purpose or that He was the Messiah the Jews were waiting for.

As I've already demonstrated, there is a religious aspect to all UFO and visitor phenomena. Almost inevitably, contactees become interested in the occult, begin to develop psychic powers, and start having out-of-body experiences.

Furthermore, these space beings bring word to us that we stand accepted in the sight of God, whoever we are, whatever we have done. "You're okay," they say. "You are not sinners, and you have no need of a sacrifice to make you right with God. You are already immortal, and you don't need to do a single thing to obtain eternal life."

But Jesus clearly said that His death was to atone for the sins of mankind. This stands in stark contrast to the teachings of visitors from space. The impact that Christ's teachings have had on humankind can't be ignored or swept under the rug—but those involved in the struggle for human souls will have won a major victory if they can turn the Gospel to their own advantage.

Al Bender was told by his visitors that there was

---

5. *The Urantia Book*, 2002.

SO SOMEBODY'S LYING—BUT WHY?

no afterlife and that Jesus Christ was no more than a mortal with an extraordinary belief in Jehovah. But even though Bender reported these words, he expressed his own difficulty in believing they were true.

Some people may be quick to believe that Jesus was just a man, but millions of others have been touched by Jesus Christ and could not for a single minute believe that He was simply an ordinary human being.

What better way to discredit Jesus than by agreeing that He was someone great but at the same time planting the seed of a thought that He wasn't divine?

Earlier I mentioned my experiences with a Ouija board, a device alleged to contact the spirits of the dead, a practice prohibited by the Bible.

One of the first times I ever used the device, I asked it—or rather the spirit behind it—to tell me the name of the most important person who had ever lived. Without hesitation, the planchette spelled "Jesus Christ."

I was a bit taken aback. Even though the answer was the one I had hoped for, I hadn't expected it. But because the board acknowledged the importance (though not the divinity) of Christ, I felt comforted and encouraged, as if I could trust the force controlling the planchette on the board. I didn't realize at the time that even the demons often acknowledge the importance of Christ. They have to do that because He made such a profound impact on our planet. Their trick is to pretend to honor and revere Christ, even while demoting Him to the ranks of "a great teacher," or even "one of the enlightened ones."

SO SOMEBODY'S LYING—BUT WHY?

The Urantia Book explains that the Person known on earth as Jesus Christ was in reality "the Universe Sovereign, Michael of Nebadon." It is tempting to dismiss *The Urantia Book* as the product of paranoid delusions, except for the occasional passages when the incredibly complicated and obtuse language gives way to straightforward clarity.

Dr. William Sadler, in his book titled *The Mind at Mischief*, lashed out at psychic fads and explained away automatic writing and other paranormal activities as either out-and-out frauds or subconscious tricks of the mind. But then he referred readers to an appendix "for a brief notice of a very unusual case of supposedly automatic writing associated with other psychic phenomena which came under my observation many years go."[6] In this appendix, Dr. Sadler wrote about his experiences with the "channel" through which *The Urantia Book* was delivered:

> A thorough study of this case has convinced me that it is not one of ordinary trance.... At no time during the period of eighteen years' observation has there been a communication from any source that claimed to be the spirit of a deceased human being. The communications which have been written, or which we have had the opportunity to hear spoken, are made by a vast order of alleged beings who claim to come from other planets to visit this world, to stop here as student visitors for

---
6. Quoted in Vallee, *Messengers of Deception*, 125.

SO SOMEBODY'S LYING—BUT WHY?

study and observation when they are en route from one universe to another.... Much of the material secured through this subject is quite contrary to his habits of thought, to the way in which he has been taught, and to his entire philosophy.... I have found in these years of observation that all the information imparted through this source has proved to be consistent within itself.

In other words, there is an intelligence behind *The Urantia Book*. It isn't gibberish, and as far as a distinguished psychologist was able to tell, it was not the product of a schizophrenic mind. Some of it, however, is almost impossible to understand.

In the mid-seventies, a friend of mine surrendered his life to one of the popular Indian god-king-gurus. My friend transformed his house into an ashram. Huge pictures of the "enlightened one" stared from every wall. Guests were requested to remove their shoes before entering the house, just as God instructed Moses to remove his shoes at the site of the burning bush because he was standing on holy ground.

My friend and I had numerous discussions about our religious differences. To get him to read some of my Christian materials, I agreed to read several tracts containing the revelations of his New Age god.

I was amazed to discover that this brilliant teacher was totally indecipherable. He simply didn't make sense! His words sounded so lofty and wise—but when I stopped to ask what they meant I came up empty.

When I talked to my friend about this, I learned

SO SOMEBODY'S LYING—BUT WHY?

that he took comfort in the complexity and near incoherency of his guru's words. Here was teaching and truths too exalted for mere mortals to grasp. The fact that no one could understand a thing he was talking about added to this god-king's credibility.

How unlike Jesus, who presented the most complex truths of the universe in simple stories about everyday occurrences.

These high-sounding, complicated words have a comforting, numbing effect that almost hypnotize us into believing them. And so we get teachings such as these in *The Urantia Book*:

> On returning from superuniverse service, a Havona Servital may enjoy numerous divine embraces and emerge therefrom merely an exalted servital. Experiencing the luminous embrace does not necessarily signify that the servital must translate into a Graduate Guide, but almost one quarter of those who achieve the divine embrace never return to the service of the realms.[7]

There are references throughout the book to the Melchizedeks or Melchizedek sons, who are among the highest leaders of the cosmos. The Book of Genesis records that Abraham met a king named Melchizedek after he had defeated Kedorlaomer and the others kings who had been allied with him.

Then Melchizedek king of Salem brought out

---
7. *The Urantia Book*, 271.

bread and wine. He was priest of God Most High, and he blessed Abram, saying, "Blessed be Abram by God Most High, Creator of heaven and earth. And blessed be God Most High, who delivered your enemies into your hand." Then Abram gave him a tenth of everything.   Genesis 14:18–20

Another brief biblical reference to Melchizedek is found in the Psalms, where David writes of a promise that God has made to the Messiah: "The Lord has sworn and will not change his mind: 'You are a priest forever, in the order of Melchizedek' " (Psalm 110:4).

This is a vague reference to Melchizedek's importance. Hebrews 7 also discusses the importance of this mysterious king. But neither gives him the status he seems to enjoy within the world of the mystical.

According to *The Urantia Book*, "Melchizedek Sons serve in many unique capacities. It is easily possible for such a son to make himself visible to mortal beings, and sometimes one of this order has even incarnated in the likeness of mortal flesh."

The book goes on to say that the "Melchizedek" who appeared to Abram had chosen to incarnate because he wanted to bring religious enlightenment—the knowledge that there is only one God at the heart and center of the universe.

Some claim that the development of all world religions came about because of these Melchizedek messengers, and that certain messengers spent time in Italy six hundred years before Christ was born, paving the way for the acceptance of Christianity there. The name Melchizedek shows up often in occult literature and plays a prominent role in the theology of the Mormon church, which has two levels of priesthood, the higher one known as the priesthood of Melchizedek.

There are secret societies that call themselves by Melchizedek's name, and he is considered a symbol of power and mystery.

UFO authority Jacques Vallee has looked into some of these organizations. In California's Silicon Valley, eleven young men and women were "initiated" into the Order of Melchizedek as they were baptized in a hot tub. In Illinois, a group called STELLE was started, "which derives its entire philosophy from Melchizedek, whom they believe to preside over 'the Archangelic Host of our Solar System,' helped by billions of Masters from the planet Klarian."[8]

A Melchizedek devotee by the name of Jim Hurtak told Vallee that "The Order of Melchizedek is one of the higher orders of the various Space Brotherhoods. There are 70 such Brotherhoods that comprise the Sons of Light, or the White Brotherhood, as it is known in some popular literature in our particular local universe. . . . If we look at the historical documents which acknowledge that, along with the appearance of UFOs, there is the bringing of a cosmic law, which is distinct from those which do not bring a spiritual teaching. The more advanced extraterrestrials do not look differently

---

8. Vallee, *Messengers of Deception*, 132.

from humans, with the facial features of biological societies that somehow are part of the same galactic tree of knowledge."[9]

And so these UFOnauts, whoever they may be, are about to usher in a new cosmic law, or at least to bring us to a deeper spiritual understanding. Apparently what we have right now is not good enough.

Hurtak claims he came to understand all of this as a result of an encounter with a spaceship. He was driving down the highway with two passengers in his car when he noticed a light following him. He pulled over to the side of the road and waited. The light turned out to be a spacecraft that landed within a few hundred feet of his car. It imparted knowledge to him via a beam of light that went through his body.

He told Vallee, "I believe that the Earth will be contacted within the next 18 months by highly evolved intelligent beings from other worlds. This belief has come about as a result of a study of prophetic literature, claimed UFO contacts, recent forecasts, and countless other materials."[10]

Hurtak made that statement more than ten years ago, and we're still waiting.

So what else is new?

Even though these people are being deceived on some points, they are intelligent men and women—some of them with important positions in the scientific

---

9. Vallee, *Messengers of Deception*, 135.
10. Vallee, *Messengers of Deception*, 132.

and academic communities. They are tuned in to voices from somewhere. They are not making all this up.

Vallee, a no-nonsense astrophysicist who doesn't believe any of this business about Melchizedek and *The Urantia Book*, has this to say:

> *The Book of Urantia* contains a surprisingly clear and readable section on religious history, and many inspired passages on morality and ethics. These sections are in striking contrast to the childish descriptions of the Spheres of the Beyond, which the imagination of the author has populated with beings that would not survive in the pages of the most grotesque piece of science fiction.

Although not a believer, Vallee admits having had an experience in Los Angeles that was almost too unusual to be coincidental:

> I had to get to KABC on La Cienega Boulevard for a radio interview. I looked at the traffic coming toward me, and saw several taxicabs a block away. I raised my hand. A car swerved out of the mainstream and came to the curb. We drove to the station, without once discussing my current research, and I got a receipt from the driver. The shock came two days later when I took the receipt from my wallet. It was signed Melchizedek! ...
>
> Perhaps I am becoming superstitious. This incident happened the week when I started writing this book, collecting all my notes about the Melchizedek groups. Most coincidences you can

rationalize away. I tried to rationalize this one away. I couldn't.[11]

As proof of this strange "coincidence," Vallee presented a photostat of the receipt given to him by the cab driver named Melchizedek.

Was it a coincidence, or was a well-organized intelligence at work here?

The evidence indicates that the latter is true.

WHO IS "I AM"?

There are other areas where the UFO people try to put a spin on biblical teachings to make them conform to the beliefs of the New Age.

Consider the Bible's references to "I AM."

When Moses encountered the burning bush and heard God's call to go into Egypt to set the Israelites free, he was reluctant to go (Exodus 3:13, 14).

> Moses said to God, "Suppose I go to the Israelites and say to them, 'The God of your fathers has sent me to you,' and they ask me, 'What is his name?' Then what shall I tell them?"
>
> God said to Moses, "I AM Who I AM. This is what you are to say to the Israelites: 'I AM has sent me to you.'"

In this way, God explained His eternal majesty. He was THE preexistent God, and that was all Moses or the Israelites needed to know at that time.

---

11. Vallee, *Messengers of Deception*, 210.

The idea of "I AM" has been appropriated by the "space beings" and given an entirely new meaning. In more of the "you are god" talk, I AM is said to refer to the power that lies within all human beings.

In *Aliens Among Us*, Ruth Montgomery presents the teachings of a young man named John Andreadis, who, she says, came to be born on earth to teach us, even though his native planet is in the region of the star Arcturus.

This sort of talk sounds silly, but Ruth Montgomery apparently believes it, and so, I presume, do many of the thousands or perhaps even millions of people who read her books. Montgomery says that her guides told her that "each of us is something of God, and that we are all one. Together we form God, and it is therefore essential that we help each other, so that all may advance together."[12]

She then quotes Andreadis:

> We realize that all apparent individuals are only expressions of one individual—I AM. This I AM is life. It is pure unqualified energy, and whenever the I AM contacts matter, the matter is activated and comes alive. Thus, because our space friends and the ascended masters exhibit a greater degree of I AM identification than most humans, they inhabit higher vibrational worlds and are able to live in multidimensional consciousness. Their presence proves that souls were not meant to be

---

12. Montgomery, *Aliens Among Us*, 139.

bound in the physical vibrations of any planet; but if they realize who they are, they can manifest perfect freedom...."[13]

He goes on in this fashion for several more pages, acknowledging along the way that God is the supreme I AM.

This is all very seductive, and up to a certain point it is in keeping with the teachings of the Bible. After all, Genesis does tell us that we were created in God's image, implying that we have something of God within us. But it is taking a giant step over the line to say that we are "I AM, the uncreated, silent watcher."

We are not and never will be capable of obtaining any sort of equality with the eternal I AM, and it is only through the atonement offered in the sacrifice of Christ that we are able to come into His presence.

In the Genesis account of humanity's fall from grace, what did the serpent say to Adam and Eve?

> The woman said to the serpent, "We may eat fruit from the trees in the garden, but God did say, 'You must not eat fruit from the tree that is in the middle of the garden, and you must not touch it, or you will die.'"
>
> "You will not surely die," the serpent said to the woman. "For God knows that when you eat of it your eyes will be opened, and you will be like God...." Genesis 3:3–5

---

13. Montgomery, *Aliens Among Us*, 167–178.

SO SOMEBODY'S LYING—BUT WHY?

That was the first deception, the first occasion when Satan gave the Word of God a slight twist to make it more palatable to us human beings. The serpent lied because, for reasons of his own, he wanted to see mankind fall into disgrace.

We would all do well to remember that serpents come in many forms, and they are still twisting eternal truths to suit their purposes. They give us new "holy books" to supplement or replace the Bible. They tell us that Jesus was a great Teacher, but that His death on the cross had no deeper meaning than that a good and innocent man was killed by an angry mob. And they tell us we are gods.

Why are they lying to us like this?

It's not likely that they are doing it out of love and respect for humankind. There is a war going on in our universe, a to-the-death battle between the forces of good and evil.

All is not peace and harmony in the cosmos. There are bad guys out there—and they're doing their best to convince us they are really the good guys.

This war isn't over land or ideology. It's being fought for the souls of men.

We will go to the victors.

Chapter Six

WHY ARE THEY HERE?

On a windy, chilly March morning a call came in to the Cochran County, Texas, sheriff's department from an irate rancher. Something had been killing his cattle, and he wanted the sheriff's department to investigate.

"Something? What do you mean by something?" the sheriff wanted to know. "Was it an animal—a coyote perhaps?"

"No," the rancher replied. "Nothing of the sort. My cattle are being butchered by someone who drops out of the sky to get them."

The sheriff wasn't sure what he was getting into, but in a matter of minutes he was on his way to the scene.

When he arrived at the ranch, the rancher took him to a spot in a field about two miles from the house. There the sheriff saw what the rancher had been talking about.

WHY ARE THEY HERE?

A perfectly round circle, about thirty feet across, had been formed in the field, as if some great, heavy, circular machine had come out of the sky and landed on the spot. And there, lying in the middle of the circle was a dead cow.

Closer examination revealed that the animal had been butchered with incredibly sharp and fine instruments. The cow's jaw had been cut back and her tongue removed. There were other incisions in the carcass, including one where the navel had been completely cut out.

Whoever did this had no interest in beef as food, because nothing with any food value had been taken, with the exception of the tongue.

What's more, the cow probably had not been butchered on this spot, because there was no blood on the ground—or on the cow. This had been a nice, neat job—although completely bizarre and unreasonable.

What purpose could anyone have for butchering a cow like this? Did someone take delight in inflicting pain on a helpless animal? How did the person come and go without being seen? And how did the circle get there, and how did it relate to the cow's death?

Then the sheriff remembered another rancher who said his cattle had been killed. Was there another carcass?

In a wheat field just a quarter-mile away was another butchered animal—a steer—lying within another large circle. This time there was something else, almost as strange as the mutilation itself. Within the circle, the

WHY ARE THEY HERE?

wheat had been burned down to within about four inches of the ground, as if a huge ball of fire had come out of the sky and *almost* touched the ground. Almost, but not quite; otherwise the wheat would have been burned completely to the ground.

The sheriff had no explanation for these strange happenings, which soon attracted the attention of officials at Reese Air Force Base, who sent a team to investigate.

The team turned up nothing unusual. The large circles did not give off abnormally high doses of radiation, and the investigators found no additional physical evidence to indicate that anything unusual had happened in Cochran County. Nothing but those dead animals and strange circles.

And something else, too.

Several residents of the area reported seeing strange lights in the sky during the days immediately before and after the cattle mutilations. According to their report, "The people that have been reporting this all tell the same story. 'It' is about as wide as a two-lane highway, round and looks the color of the sun when it is going down."[1]

Nobody ever did figure out what had happened near the tiny Texas town of Whiteface, but there were all sorts of rumors.

Some said the cattle had been butchered by

---

1. Cochran County, Texas, sheriff's report of March 10, 1975, quoted in Vallee, *Messengers of Deception*, 168.

WHY ARE THEY HERE?

Satanists who used the blood and other organs in satanic rituals. Some rumors said certain helicopter pilots were selling animal organs to occultic groups. They would drop out of the sky to pick up the hapless animal, butcher it, and then drop it back to the ground.

Others said the air force didn't get to the bottom of these incidents because it was behind them. They figured the military had killed the cattle to test some new drug or weapon.

A third group suspected the killings were the work of extraterrestrials—although why they had butchered the animals was anybody's guess. Perhaps to learn something about the way life had evolved on earth, or maybe because they needed some particular enzyme or other animal product.

The happenings in Cochran County were not isolated incidents. Cattle mutilations started occurring throughout the western United States and as far north as Canada. Sometimes the mutilations occurred along with those large, circular indentions, and sometimes they didn't—but all the animals were stabbed to death with very sharp instruments and had various organs removed. A number of different organs were involved. Sometimes the eyes were taken from their sockets. Occasionally an ear would be removed. The sex organs might be cut off. Or the blood would be completely drained. And all sorts of animals became victims—cows, sheep, pigs, and poultry of various types.

On one occasion a mutilated steer was found to have all four legs broken in an impact-style injury, as if

WHY ARE THEY HERE?

the animal's carcass had been dropped from a significant height.

One farmer found the carcass of a mutilated pig within two hundred yards of his house. The lights had gone off, and when he went outside to investigate he found the dead pig. There were many other pigs in the pen going about their routine, and they had not made a big enough fuss to alert the farmer that something was wrong. The farmer had heard nothing—not the sound of an intruder, nor one single squealing noise from a pig in trouble—although he told investigators he knew firsthand what sort of a racket a pig makes when it is being slaughtered.

At Colorado's Cheyenne Mountain Zoo, a 1500-pound female buffalo was mutilated. An udder, an ear, and several square feet of the animal's hide had been removed.

El Paso County Coroner Dr. Raoul W. Urich said, "The cutting was done neatly, cleanly, obviously with a very sharp cutting instrument. The dissection was of the type that would eliminate any type of predator." He added, "It was better than I could do if I were trying. It was really an expert job."[2]

Snuggled up next to Cheyenne Mountain—and even within the mountain—is Ent Air Force Base, headquarters for the North American Air Defense Command and the Canadian Air Defense Command. It holds the most sensitive equipment on the North American con-

---

2. *Colorado Springs Sun*, October 23, 1975.

WHY ARE THEY HERE?

tinent, supposedly keeping watch over our skies to make sure our air space is not invaded. Yet intruders had dropped out of the sky into the Cheyenne Mountain Zoo, slaughtered a buffalo, and left the scene the same way they had come. Right under the nose of NORAD. And nobody saw a thing.

The situation got so bad in Colorado that the governor, Richard D. Lamm, met in a special session with the executive board of the state cattlemen's association. He told them that the mutilations represented "one of the greatest outrages in the history of the western cattle industry." He added that it was "no longer possible to blame predators for the mutilations."[3]

That was certainly true. It would take a gigantic leap of logic to blame all of this on wolves, coyotes, or mountain lions! It seems more likely that somebody was sending a message to the United States and to the rest of the world, a message that said, "We can come and go as we like. We can do whatever we like. And there's not the least thing you can do to stop us."

Something sinister was happening out there, and the combined efforts of the best law enforcement and military agencies couldn't do a thing to stop it.

One member of the Colorado Bureau of Investigation said that trying to catch whoever was responsible was like trying to catch a ghost. But something more substantial than a ghost was involved. The butchered carcasses gave silent testimony to that fact.

---

3. *Meeker* (Colorado) *Herald*, September 6, 1975.

WHY ARE THEY HERE?

Ghost lights may dance in the twilight sky. Ghostly images may float on the wind and disappear into nothingness when you reach out to them. A ghost may moan and groan and rattle chains in the middle of the night. But a ghost can't cut up a 1500-pound buffalo with speed and precision that would make a surgeon jealous.

Those responsible for the mutilations must have been solid physical persons the same as you and I. They may have been doing the bidding of someone who remained behind the scenes, unseen and undetectable. And there may have been some force involved that allowed them to do their dirty work without detection, but that is speculation. It is also speculation that the cattle mutilations had something to do with the glowing balls seen flying through the skies around the time and place where they took place. But most residents of those areas were pretty quick to say they believed there was a connection.

Reports of cattle mutilations also came in from Europe. France, in particular, was hit hard. Some $40,000 worth of cattle were slaughtered in a few weeks. In spite of searches and all-night watches conducted by ranchers, police, and troops from the French army, the killings went on for several months, and the perpetrators were never caught.[4]

Whoever was responsible for the killings was very powerful and had international reach.

Jacques Vallee was among those who investigated

---
4. Vallee, *Messengers of Deception*, 170, 171.

the mutilations. He had been involved in UFO research for many years and had written six books and dozens of magazine articles on the subject.

Dr. Vallee is no kook. He holds a master's degree in astrophysics from a French university and a Ph.D. in computer science from Northwestern University. Before starting his own computer company he served as manager of information systems at Stanford University. He addressed the United Nations on the subject of UFOs and, as I mentioned before, he was the model for the character of LaCombe in the film *Close Encounters of the Third Kind*.

Vallee has never spoken with people from Venus or Mars. He has never gone around yelling "cover-up" and demanding that the U.S. Air Force tell us all it knows about flying saucers, nor has he been among those who attempted to explain away large metallic disks flying in an evening sky as "swamp gas" or flocks of geese.

He is diligent and scientific in his approach to UFO investigation. He isn't one of those who wants so badly to believe in UFOs that he'll accept the most preposterous story at face value. Neither is he the type who would refuse to believe it if a flying saucer landed in his own backyard—and he acknowledges that there are many UFO researchers who fit one of those categories. Dr. Vallee's years of research into UFO reports have led him to one conclusion: The UFOs are real.

He has no idea what they are or where they come from, but they are out there flying through the skies of

WHY ARE THEY HERE?

America and every other nation. Thousands of credible people have seen them—people with nothing to gain by making up stories or exaggerating their experiences. In some instances, the same objects have been seen by twenty, thirty, or more people, all of whom gave the same basic descriptions of the incident.

There are so many pieces of the puzzle that fit together that Vallee concluded there are "aliens" in our skies, and that the government isn't hiding anything because the government doesn't have a clue as to what these "spaceships" are.

If the governments of the world are covering anything up, Dr. Vallee decided, it is the fact that they don't know what's going on. He concluded that some governments act as if they know more than they do so their citizens will feel better about those strange objects zipping through their skies.

Researching the cattle mutilations was as baffling as any experience Vallee had encountered. Until this, authorities had always said UFOs left behind no physical evidence. But here it was by the truckload, and the clues led absolutely nowhere.

For Vallee, this was one more piece of a puzzle that was beginning to take definite shape in his mind. When he first began looking into the phenomenon of UFOs he believed that if they were real they would turn out to be interplanetary spacecraft—nothing more and nothing less.

Although Vallee was more convinced than ever that the saucers were real, he wasn't feeling so certain that

WHY ARE THEY HERE?

their point of origin was outer space. He wrote, "I had become aware of some pretty shady business behind the apparently harmless antics of the contactee groups. Now I wanted to focus my attention on the problem at hand: the question of who was doing all this and what their designs on us might be."[5]

Just what sort of "shady business" had Vallee discovered?

OUT TO TAKE OVER THE WORLD

Over the years, Vallee talked to many UFO cultists who believed they alone held the key to changing this world into what it was meant to be, and they were ready to do what they could to usher in the "New Age."

They were, in short, interested in taking control of the planet. They talked about a unified, one-world government that would put an end to centuries of wars and rumors of wars. A new economic system would be established in which money would be eliminated and all people everywhere would share equally in the planet's wealth.

All political parties and such "outmoded" ways of choosing leaders as holding elections would be eliminated for the sake of worldwide unity. (Apparently aliens are better qualified than we are to say who our leaders should be.)

A new worldwide religion would be ushered in, revealing the real nature of the universe and sweeping

---

5. Vallee, *Messengers of Deception*, 137.

WHY ARE THEY HERE?

away all the false notions we have about eternal truth. Presumably this would mean the crumbling of all current world religions, including Islam, Buddhism, Hinduism, Judaism, and, of course, Christianity.

The UFO cultists and contact groups are still small in number and seemingly insignificant. They can talk all they want to about bringing in a new world order, but they can't do it with an army of only a few thousand. But that army is growing. On the periphery are thousands hearing the message being spread by the UFO groups. They are being conditioned to think, feel, and react in new ways.

Jesus Christ started out with only twelve apostles. But those men turned the entire world upside down. And on the other side of the coin, Hitler quickly went from being considered a crackpot to establishing himself as the sole ruler of Germany.

Those on the periphery may not be sure that aliens exist, but they haven't ruled it out. And if a landing of an alien spacecraft shows up on the eleven o'clock news some night, they won't be terribly surprised, nor perhaps terribly upset.

It's not as if human beings were slaughtered in the same way as cattle and other animals, so whoever was responsible at least made a distinction between the murder of a human and the slaughter of an animal. As long as the animals weren't tortured, was it really so terrible? After all, cows and steers are killed in slaughterhouses every day.

And yet they've left a sinister message: "Look what

we've been able to get away with. And if we can get away with this, just think what else we might be able to do."

They wow us with their wisdom and love. Then they show us they can get away with murder if they want to. They want us to stand in awe of them, to welcome them with open arms, but apparently it serves their purposes to have us fear them too, at least a little bit.

Jacques Vallee has admitted that his own conclusions about UFOs may have set him at odds with his colleagues. But he is confident of his conclusions:

> I don't think we should expect salvation from the sky.
>
> I think we have a very real UFO problem. I have also come to believe that it is being manipulated for political ends. And the data suggest that the manipulators may be human beings with a plan for social control. Such plans have been made before, and have succeeded. History shows that having a cosmic mythology as part of such a plan is not always necessary. But it certainly helps.[6]

* * *

Let me summarize my conclusions thus far. UFOs are real. They are an application of psychotronic technology; that is, they are physical devices used to affect human consciousness. They may not be

---
6. Vallee, *Messengers of Deception*, 157.

WHY ARE THEY HERE?

from outer space; they may, in fact, be terrestrial-based manipulating devices. Their purpose may be to achieve social changes on this planet. Their methods are those of deception: systematic manipulation of witnesses and contactees; covert use of various sects and cult control of the channels through which the alleged "space messages" can make an impact on the public.[7]

Why did Vallee come to the conclusion that someone is out to manipulate us? He has several reasons, which I will list here, along with my elaborations.

1. There have been too many sightings.

If the UFO people want to come and go without being noticed, they're not doing a very good job of it. In fact, it looks as if they want us to see them.

Since Kenneth Arnold coined the term *flying saucers* in 1947, there have been thousands upon thousands of reported sightings. Vallee has calculated that if all the reports of UFO landings are accurate, there have been more than 3 million on this planet over the last twenty years. That's too many, he says, to support the theory that the UFOs are piloted by space beings making a general survey of our planet.

What's more, UFOs have been sighted over heavily populated areas. They have buzzed busy highways. They have landed near mining sites where men were obviously working. Why aren't they more careful if they don't want to be seen?

---

7. Vallee, *Messengers of Deception*, 21.

WHY ARE THEY HERE?

2. UFOs do things that aren't possible according to our understanding of physics.

One witness reported seeing two UFOs heading toward each other at an incredibly high rate of speed. They kept coming and coming. Finally they hit. But there was no explosion. Simply a merging of the two craft into one larger one.

Other craft have made ninety-degree turns in an instant. A UFO was traveling along, parallel to the ground, at a speed estimated in excess of six hundred miles an hour. Then suddenly it was going straight up at the same rate of speed. Did the occupants have to peel themselves off the ceiling of their craft after a maneuver like that?

Some UFOs have simply vanished.

Physical craft could not do these things, but images could—whether they were produced by holographic projection or hypnotic suggestion.

3. Most UFO sightings take place at night.

The witnesses see lights flashing across the sky. It's much easier for someone to play tricks on an unsuspecting public under cover of darkness.

Here, as in every other instance, the most important question concerns the motivations behind these alarming visions.

Are the visitors interested in setting us free from our problems? Or are they focusing on our problems to convince us that their way is our only hope for overcoming them?

They come to us as scolding parents, saying, "Look

at the mess you've made of things. Now, watch us, and we'll show you how things ought to be done."

Why not believe them? If they've been around as long as they say they have, they ought to have all the answers.

SOCIAL CONSEQUENCES OF BELIEF IN UFOs

When Dr. Vallee began his research into unidentified objects, he believed that if there was any truth to their existence it would be the obvious one—that UFOs were physical machines piloted by beings from other planets. But the more he looked into UFO and alien-contact reports, the more convinced he became that someone wanted to alter our society. He believes there are at least six social effects that a belief in UFOs is bringing to our society.

1. Belief in UFOs will widen the gap between public and scientific institutions.

2. The contactee propaganda undermines the image of human beings as masters of their own destiny.

3. Increased attention given to UFO activity promotes the concept of political unification of this planet.

4. Contactee organizations may become the basis of a new "high demand" religion.

5. Irrational motivations based on faith are spreading hand in hand with the belief in extraterrestrial intervention.

6. Contactee philosophies often include belief in

higher races and in totalitarian systems that would eliminate democracy.[8]

Taking a closer look at these six statements, it's easy to see the truth behind each of them—and why each of these occurrences can mean dangerous changes in our society. Let me elaborate:

> 1. *Belief in UFOs will widen the gap between the public and scientific institutions.*

A man in Alabama sees a huge metallic disk zooming through the sky, traveling faster than any aircraft he's ever seen. But when he reports the incident, investigating scientists tell him he saw a runaway weather balloon.

A group of people in Texas pull their cars off to the side of the road to watch several very bright lights flying in close formation. Later they hear the official explanation for what they saw and learn they were simply "confused by the unusual brightness of the planet Venus."

The man in Alabama doesn't know for sure what he saw, but he's certain it wasn't any weather balloon. The folks in Texas are indignant too, because they know the difference between a series of lights traveling at a high rate of speed and a stationary planet.

If this sort of thing continues, it won't be long until the attitude of the general public is that our governmental and scientific authorities either are lying to us or they really don't know what's going on. If they refuse to tell the truth about UFOs, why trust them about anything?

---
8. Vallee, *Messengers of Deception*, 217–219.

WHY ARE THEY HERE?

And if science belittles our experiences with UFOs and visitors, refusing to take them seriously, sooner or later we'll turn the tables and refuse to take traditional science seriously.

We are beyond thinking that science will conquer all of our problems and provide answers to all our questions. But still, within the boundaries of religious faith, we believe pretty much of what scientists tell us about the world and universe. Take away that belief and we create a vacuum.

Nature abhors a vacuum; something will quickly move into that empty space to fill it up. As we discard old scientific realities, new ones will take their place, even if these new "realities" are nothing more than lies, fables, and superstitions.

> 2. *The contactee propaganda undermines the image of human beings as masters of their own destiny.*

Christians already know that humans have never really been in charge of their destinies. Our lives are in God's hands, as is the existence of our universe.

But even though we know the future depends entirely on God, we also know that He has called us into a partnership with Him. He expects us to work at solving our own problems—to preserve our environment, to work for social justice, to feed the hungry, lift up the fallen, and so on. Those who believe in Christ know He will work through us and with us to solve our problems, but He's not going to do everything for us.

WHY ARE THEY HERE?

Those who look for salvation to come via the visitors seem to believe we can't do anything at all unless the Space Brothers intervene on our behalf.

Furthermore, it's one thing to depend on God, who has revealed Himself to humans through history, and something else to depend on visitors who won't tell us who they are or why they're here.

Time after time throughout history, men and women have put blind faith in a leader only to have him betray their trust as soon as he acquires power.

Contactees put absolute faith in those they know absolutely nothing about. And doing so is always dangerous.

3. Increased attention given to UFO activity promotes the concept of political unification of this planet.

Planet earth will never be able to take its rightful place in the Federation of Planets (or whatever universal government there might be) until we have become unified ourselves. How can our Space Brothers welcome us into their fellowship while we are still fighting with each other?

There are many groups that yearn to establish a one-world, utopian government. This isn't the province of the UFO groups alone, but they are at the forefront of those calling for all borders to be erased and for the world to come together under the banner of one central government.

It's a nice dream. How wonderful to see an end to

WHY ARE THEY HERE?

nationalism, to have the whole world covered with a blanket of peace. It's not likely to happen without the intervention of some outside force, and contactee groups believe that force is at hand and ready to take action.

Here again, a primary question is whether the forces at work here have the ultimate benefit of mankind in mind or if they're preparing to control our society—whether that control is psychological, intellectual, political, or spiritual.

In *The UFO Abductors*, Brad Steiger tells stories of many men and women who are convinced they don't belong on this planet. They believe they came here from other galaxies for some purpose, and they are waiting for this purpose to be revealed to them.

These people were born here—there's plenty of proof of that. This is an instance when belief in UFOs and contact with aliens is bound up in reincarnation and "past lives." They believe they are on earth for this particular life span, but that their real homes are among the stars. "In the fulness of time" it will be revealed to them why they were "incarnated" onto the earth. Others of them believe their mothers are "earth women" and their fathers are from "the stars."

Do I believe these people are correct in believing they have been brought here from space? Of course not.

But they believe it—and believe it so strongly that they say they are willing to do whatever their space parents tell them.

Are these people out-and-out loonies? Were they

never able to "fit in," so they developed fantasies to make themselves feel worthwhile? Or has someone deceived them into believing they are from the stars—someone who is putting together an army through every means possible. It's much easier to topple an empire if you have taken steps to erode it from within.

In *The Manchurian Candidate*, a hypnotic suggestion is implanted within a man's brain. He appears perfectly normal, but when he hears a particular word he is programmed to go into a trancelike state and do everything within his power to assassinate an important political leader.

He thinks his life belongs to him and that his actions are his own, but he's mistaken. He's really under the control of a sinister foreign power.

Brad Steiger, who would seem to believe UFOs are real and primarily friendly, says that "an army of men and women could be ready to take action that they themselves do not even understand—yet they would have no option other than to obey when the prearranged signal was given. Their reaction would be as those individuals who are under deep hypnosis. They would obey simply because they had been conditioned to obey at a prearranged signal."[9]

Then Steiger quotes UFOlogist and author John Keel, who writes:

> We have no way of knowing how many human beings throughout the world may have been

---

9. Steiger, *The UFO Abductors*, 205.

processed in this manner, as they would have absolutely no memory of undergoing the experience; and so we have no way of determining who among us has strange and sinister "programs" lying dormant in the dark corners of his mind.[10]

"Suppose the plan is to process millions of people and then at some future date trigger all of these minds at one time. Would we suddenly have a world of saints or would we have a world of armed maniacs shooting at one another from bell towers?"[11]

There are similar questions about the united world the visitors want to give us. Would it be a world brought together in peace, love, and harmony, or one forced together through fear and violence?

4. Contactee organizations may become the basis of a new "high demand" religion.

An acquaintance of mine, exasperated by my belief in the Bible, asked me, "What are you going to believe—a book that's thousands of years old, or something that's happening right now?"

"I'll stick with the old Book," I answered.

But millions of others will quickly exchange the old and familiar for the new and exciting.

God? He's old stuff.

Space Brothers? Wow! What a concept!

The unfortunate truth is that in too many instances the Christian church has fossilized. The God it presents

---

10. Keel, *Operation Trojan Horse*, 290.
11. Steiger, *The UFO Abductors*, 149, 150.

seems as old and dusty as most Bibles, not an active, dynamic Person who is very much involved in the world today. It's no wonder that so many people turn away from traditional religious beliefs and look to outer space instead of heaven for spiritual guidance.

Enlightened people have tried for centuries to do away with the need for religion. Religion has been denounced as a superstitious relic that would disappear as we advanced scientifically and intellectually.

The Communist system went so far as to take an official stand against religion, calling it "the opiate of the people" and looking for various ways to punish those who clung to religious belief.

And yet, in spite of the severest persecution, Christianity, Judaism, and Islam prospered and grew stronger behind the Iron Curtain.

People always have had and always will have a spiritual nature. We hunger after eternal truth.

If you wanted people to turn their backs on God you could do it one of two ways: (1) You could try to convince them He doesn't exist; (2) If that failed, you could invent a new religion and draw their allegiance to it. If successful you would have accomplished your task.

Is this what someone is trying to do?

In the Old Testament, the mark of a true prophet was that all he prophesied came to pass. If it didn't, he was marked as a false prophet. Not many people went around making up prophecies off the top of their heads. There was a severe penalty for falsely prophesying—namely, death by stoning.

WHY ARE THEY HERE?

People knew that if God was behind a prophecy it would come true. Time was and is the perfect judge of any religious movement.

The leaders of the new UFO religions have given us many prophecies. So far we have seen none of them come to pass. But still, the ranks of this new techno-religion continue to grow at a rapid rate.

People need to believe something, and once we make up our minds about what to believe—whether it regards religion, politics, or any other area of life—it takes a lot more than a few facts to convince us we're wrong.

There are plenty of facts to prove that the UFO religions are wrong, but those facts aren't enough to dissuade true believers.

I am not saying that anyone who has seen a UFO is a cultist, nor am I implying that anyone who has an experience with visitors has turned his back on God, or will do so.

Not at all. These experiences occur to innocent people from all walks of life, as Budd Hopkins points out in his book *Intruders*.

> Abductees are not "believers" in some religion of outer space, they are not seeking publicity or other rewards, and they are at heart, confused and frightened by their experiences, which they regard more as a profoundly unsettling problem in their lives than as any kind of advantage. These abductees are neither paranoid nor suffering from delusions of grandeur; they are honest people who

have suffered traumatic experiences they do not understand.[12]

The abductees may not even be members of the new UFO religion, but those new religions have most definitely grown up around them.

5. *Irrational motivations based on faith are spreading hand in hand with the belief in extraterrestrial intervention.*

God calls us to faith, but not to the kind of faith that is a blind leap into the darkness. Biblical faith is based on an understanding of the Word of God, personal experience, and revelation.

Faith in the Space Brothers is based primarily on desire. In the many books on UFO experiences, it's amazing how many stories are still being presented as absolute fact, years after they were proven to result from overactive imaginations.

In one instance, a journal that claims to seriously investigate UFO reports gave a breathless account of how a young coed had undergone an encounter of the sexual kind with a man from space.

It turned out that the account came from the "lampoon" version of a regular college newspaper. The whole story was a joke, and there wasn't a single shred of evidence to back it up. If the UFO magazine had done any checking at all, it would have discovered these facts and kept itself from looking so foolish. But the

---

12. Hopkins, *Intruders*, 149, 150.

WHY ARE THEY HERE?

field of UFO research is populated by people who want to believe.

There have been numerous books written from the viewpoint that someone—usually the United States government—is covering up the truth about UFOs. But there are just as many instances where evidence of hoaxes and lies has been covered up or ignored by researchers who wanted desperately to believe the accounts they were hearing.

> *6. Contactee philosophies often include belief in higher races and in totalitarian systems that would eliminate democracy.*

In his research into UFO sightings and groups, Jacques Vallee discovered two alarming tendencies:

First, most of the communication from outer space tended to be couched in totalitarian imagery. One group leader was told that democracy was obsolete. Another was told to expect a reversal of the old values.

Second, there was a tendency to believe in the superiority of some races over others. Specifically, lighter-skinned people were said to be superior to those with darker skin. In fact, some UFO material is overtly racist. Beyond that, there is the repeated implication that those who have extraterrestrial blood flowing through their veins are far superior to those who do not. The Bible says:

> When men began to increase in number on the earth and daughters were born to them, the sons of God saw that the daughters of men were beautiful, and they married any of them they chose....

WHY ARE THEY HERE?

> The Nephilim were on the earth in those days—and also afterward—when the sons of God went to the daughters of men and had children by them. They were the heroes of old, men of renown.
> Genesis 6:1, 2, 4

UFO believers such as Erich Von Daniken have explained those verses by saying that men from space came to the earth and mated with earth women, thus producing a super race of people.

As we've already seen, some people believe this type of crossbreeding is continuing today. This belief perpetuates the thinking that there are two strains of human beings on the earth today—those from "above" and those from "below." People from "above" are superior to those who have no "space blood" in their veins.

Instead of being the great equalizers of the human race, the great bringers of international peace and brotherhood, the Space Brothers may bring renewed bigotry and racial strife to our planet.

What does the Bible itself have to say about the superiority of one race over another? "There is neither Jew nor Greek, slave nor free, male nor female, for you are all one in Christ Jesus" (Galatians 3:28).

WHO DONE IT?

At the beginning of this chapter, I recounted some nightmarish scenes of animal mutilation from the American West. No one knew who did it, or why. No one was ever caught in the act, and no one was ever arrested.

There were never any telltale fingerprints or other evidence to lead authorities to a suspect. The killers came and went in complete secrecy.

People still wonder who did it, but perhaps that question is not as important as why they did it.

According to Jacques Vallee, there have always been two basic schools of thought concerning UFOs and related phenomena: (1) It's all nonsense; (2) We are being visited by beings from outer space.

But Jacques Vallee, who has spent countless hours investigating UFOs, has come to the conclusion that neither statement is true. It's not nonsense. And we are not being visited by beings from outer space.

Someone just wants us to think this is the case. Vallee says:

> If the Manipulators do exist, I certainly salute their tenacity, but I am curious about their goals. Anybody clever enough to exploit the public's expectation of UFO landings, or even to simulate an invasion from outer space, would presumably realize that human institutions are highly vulnerable to changes in our images of ourselves. It is not only the individual contactee who is manipulated, but the global image in humanity's collective psyche. One would like to know more, then, about the image of humanity such Manipulators harbor in their own minds—and in their hearts. Assuming, of course, that they do have hearts.[13]

---

13. Vallee, *Messengers of Deception*, 219, 220.

WHY ARE THEY HERE?

He concludes:

There is another system. It is sending us messengers of deception. They are not necessarily coming from nearby stars. In terms of the effect on us, it doesn't matter where they come from. I even suspect that "where" and "when" have no meaning here. How could we be alone? The black box of science has stopped ticking. People look up toward the stars in eager expectation.

Receiving a visit from outer space sounds almost as comfortable as having a God. Yet we shouldn't rejoice too soon. Perhaps we will get the visitors we deserve.[14]

---

14. Vallee, *Messengers of Deception*, 222, 223.

Chapter Seven

WHERE ARE THEY TAKING US?

A FRIEND OF MINE WAS TENSE, DEPRESSED, AND generally stressed-out. He wasn't about to jump off the nearest bridge or run away to Tahiti; he was simply having trouble handling all that life was throwing his way. He was trying his best to keep the juggling act going, but finding it harder and harder to keep all the balls in the air at the same time.

Mark was a Christian—but not a particularly strong one. He went to church once in a while, but more out of habit than for any other reason.

He was looking for a way to handle all that stress, and a co-worker suggested that he try an Eastern form of meditation. The colleague painted a glowing picture of what meditation had done for him—it had calmed him down, given him a more positive outlook, and helped him handle the frustrations of day-to-day living.

Mark figured it was worth a try. He certainly didn't have anything to lose—or so he thought. He vaguely remembered hearing that this form of meditation had some connection to mystical religion, but that wasn't any big deal to Mark. He was interested in it for his own personal benefit, not because he wanted any kind of mystical religious experience.

At first the meditation was wonderful. He felt relaxed, renewed, and invigorated. Before many weeks passed he became quite adept at it. Throughout the day, he would use his mantra and go as deeply as possible into the meditative state. He'd close the door of his office, sit back in his chair, and empty his mind of all its worries and cares. Meditation was just about the greatest thing he'd ever come across, and he wholeheartedly recommended it to his friends.

Deeper and deeper he went, until almost at will he could go so deep that he was beyond mere meditation and into some sort of trance.

And then it happened.

I don't know exactly what he saw, but it scared him half to death, and it sent him running into the arms of Christ, thus ending his experiment with meditation.

On a silent, breathless evening, all alone in the privacy of his own living room, Mark hit the bottom, or near bottom, of the meditation experience. He came face-to-face with something evil. Whether it was a vision or something real, he couldn't say.

"I was aware, immediately, that I was falling into the hands of someone that I didn't want to have his hands on me."

"Was it the devil?" I asked him.

"If it wasn't, I never want to see the devil."

"Can you describe what you saw?"

"I really have trouble talking about it except to say that it was awful."

"Why did you have the vision?"

"I have no idea. Maybe they figured I was so far gone that they had me, so they had nothing to lose by revealing themselves to me. Or maybe the Lord decided to be merciful to me and show me what I was getting myself into."

"What do you mean by 'they'?"

"The ones who are behind it all. Satan . . . his demons."

Whenever I hear something like that I'm always a bit skeptical.

I've never been a fan of preachers who try to scare people into heaven with horrifying descriptions of the tortures of hell, nor do I believe everything people tell me. But even though I don't know what or who Mark saw when he was in the depths of meditation, I do know that it had a profound effect on him. His life was changed by that experience, and today he is deeply committed to Christ. If you ask him, he'll tell you that sometimes you have to have an encounter with evil before you can discover what is truly good.

Mysticism, meditation, and other New Age and occultic practices are all part of the alien package. Whitley Strieber, for instance, has had several out-of-the-body experiences and claims that he once made his soul visible to a friend who was many miles away at the time.

If there has been a single instance of anyone's getting deeply involved in an investigation of UFOs without also getting involved in the occult, I have yet to find it. And my friend's experience with meditation shows the importance of finding out who we're dealing with before we commit ourselves to them.

There's a lot of talk these days about our country's dealings with the Soviet Union. We're told over and over that we can't trust the Russians, that all of their peace initiatives are just so much hot air. And I'm sure that in Moscow the citizens wonder if their country can really trust the United States. A certain amount of skepticism is necessary, because there's always someone ready and willing to take advantage of innocent trust.

So why would anyone trust beings who sneak into houses in the middle of the night, and who won't tell us who they are, why they're here, or where they've really come from?

Aliens told Whitley Strieber that he was their chosen one.[1] The whole idea of his being a chosen one struck him as absolutely ridiculous, as if it were some sort of joke. But when he let his captors know he didn't

---

1. Whitley Strieber, *Communion* (New York: William Morrow, 1988), 78–80.

believe them, they acted indignant—as if they couldn't believe he wouldn't believe them.

Almost at the same time Strieber saw visitors talking to a woman in a flower-print dress and reassuring her that she was their chosen one. She was easier to convince. She shouted, "Praise the Lord!" and seemed thrilled to be accorded this honor and privilege.

Betty Andreasson, a homemaker who recorded her experiences with visitors in a book titled *The Andreasson Affair*, was also told that she was a chosen one.

Perhaps the aliens have discovered a simple truth about the human species—that a little bit of flattery will go a long, long way.

THE SCREWTAPE CONNECTION

The visitors, whoever they may be, are anxious to have human beings on their side. They are not going to come sweeping out of the skies at any moment and invade the earth. They are doing their best to win us over to their point of view.

Whitley Strieber says that these alien creatures seem to be "orchestrating our awareness of them very carefully." He also recognizes that they seem to be trying for "a degree of influence or even control over us."[2]

In C. S. Lewis's masterful *The Screwtape Letters*, the experienced Uncle Screwtape had some good advice for the apprentice demon named Wormwood. He ex-

---

2. Strieber, *Communion*, 94, 95.

plains the ways that human beings may be manipulated by demons.

1. Get them to think too much about demons.
2. Get them to completely ignore demonic involvement in the world.
3. Get them to believe in a neutral force that is neither good nor evil.

Regarding that third point, Lewis wrote, "If once we can produce our perfect work—the Materialist Magician, the man, not using, but veritably worshipping what he vaguely calls 'Forces' while denying the existence of 'spirits'—then the end of the war will be in sight."[3]

Apparently Wormwood has been following his uncle's advice to perfection!

Streiber at first had a hard time making up his mind whether the creatures were evil or good. He eventually concludes that they do what they do out of overwhelming love for mankind, and he even reaches the point of believing they may be sacrificing something of themselves to help us, even though a voice once proclaimed to him, "I can do what I wish to you."[4]

That particular incident occurred when Strieber was feeling very satisfied with himself, reflecting on the success of his novels and looking with pride around the property his book royalties had enabled him to buy. At

---

3. C. S. Lewis, *The Screwtape Letters* (New York: The Macmillan Company, 1973), 33.
4. Strieber, *Transformation*, 143.

that point the voice told him he was arrogant and said, "I can do what I wish to you."

That same afternoon, Strieber found out about a problem at his bank. He had recently transferred his life savings from one institution to another—and he received word that something had gone wrong. A computer error had effectively erased the transfer. The money had vanished into thin air. Unless the mistake could be rectified, he would face financial ruin.

Strieber knew the "computer error" had been induced by the voice that had chastised him for his arrogance, and he spent a long night worrying about the situation. As it turned out the mistake was corrected the following day.

I suppose it's better to believe someone is making you suffer to teach you a lesson for your own benefit than to believe he is making you suffer merely because he enjoys seeing you squirm and because he wants to demonstrate that he has complete control over your life. And if you are powerless to stop strange creatures from invading your home night after night, certainly you'd rather see them as angels than demons. Otherwise, how could you stand the terror?

Strieber is one of many abductees who has described powerlessness in the presence of the visitors.

I have, on occasion, been partially awakened in the middle of the night and had my mind wake up but not my body. I felt as if something was sitting on my chest, pinning me to the bed. I wanted to move an arm or leg—something—just to prove to myself I was still alive. But try as I might, I couldn't get anything to move. I felt a powerful force pushing me onto the bed and back into the world of sleep. I fought it with all my strength because it seemed vitally important that I get myself out of this state. As near as I can figure out, that's pretty much what it's like to wake up and find the visitors gathered around your bed.

Being caught between waking and sleeping is a horrible feeling, and I would just as soon it never happened to me again. But imagine what it would be like to have one of those experiences—lying helpless on your bed, unable to lift even a finger to defend yourself—and be surrounded by creatures resembling gigantic praying mantises.

If you weren't sure whether the creatures were evil or good, you'd certainly hope they were on the side of the angels. And so Strieber has convinced himself that these little men and women mean us no harm, that they are here to lead us into a deeper experience of life.

And yet, as mentioned, he had a very hard time making up his mind:

> There are worse things than death, I suspected. And I was beginning to get the distinct impression that one of them had taken an interest in me.
>
> Alone at night I worried about the legendary cunning of demons.[5]

He also discusses his attempt to walk out into the

---

5. Strieber, *Transformation*, 45.

woods at night, hoping to provoke an encounter with the visitors:

> I'd never witnessed such terror in myself. My mind was frightened, but some other, deeper part of me was literally beside itself. The visitors brought terror to the blood and muscle of me, to the reptile that crouches at the bottom of every human being.
>
> Why? Did my unconscious know something about them that my conscious mind was just beginning to admit?[6]

And yet again:

> I felt an absolutely indescribable sense of menace. It was hell on earth to be there, and yet I couldn't move, couldn't cry out, couldn't get away. I lay as still as death, suffering inner agonies. Whatever was there seemed so monstrously ugly, so filthy and dark and sinister. Of course they were demons. They had to be. And they were here and I couldn't get away. I couldn't save my poor family.[7]

Strieber's terror at such moments is understandable. It's never easy to come face-to-face with the unknown, and it must be pure horror to be in the presence of an unknown being that may be capable of turning you into a midnight snack!

In some of his encounters he felt as if the negative

---
6. Strieber, *Transformation*, 124.
7. Strieber, *Transformation*, 181.

impulses of some of the creatures were being held in check by other more positive beings. They never did anything that seemed designed to harm him, really, but he got the impression that some of these guys had a severe attitude.

In acknowledging the negative nature of some of these beings, he discusses the importance of negative experiences. We all need them because they cause us to grow stronger, become wiser, develop compassion for others, and so on. If all we had was one positive experience piled on top of another, none of us would ever become anything other than shallow, self-important, spoiled brats.

Strieber's right about that of course. In the Bible, the Book of James reminds us that we should rejoice when we have trials, because those trials have come to make us more like Christ. But that's a long way from saying that anyone who attempts to harm us is really trying to help us because he knows his attempts to harm us will make us stronger.

Follow this reasoning to its logical conclusion and we come to believe there is no such thing as good and evil, only a force used to bring about personal growth.

It would be wonderful to believe in a universe where there is no such thing as out-and-out evil, but practical experience, not to mention the Word of God, tells us otherwise.

There is a great temptation to believe in a supernatural force that is neither inherently good nor evil. It's just there—a neutral, and yet incredibly powerful foun-

WHERE ARE THEY TAKING US?

tain of energy just waiting for us to tap into it. That is the idea behind "the force" in the movie *Star Wars*. Luke Skywalker used "the force" for good, while Darth Vader used it to destroy. That was fine because *Star Wars* was only a movie, but the idea of an impersonal, supernatural force is not the reality behind our universe.

Good exists, and so does evil. There is spiritual warfare in the heavenly places, and no matter how much we want it, it's impossible to be neutral. There's no such thing as a spiritual Switzerland—a place that refuses to align itself with either of the warring parties.

Like Uncle Screwtape told Wormwood, if you can get them to believe in a neutral force that is neither good nor evil, you have gained control over them.

THE CONNECTION WITH DEATH

The visitors seem to have an intimate connection with death and dying. They told Whitley Strieber they were in the business of "recycling souls."

Furthermore, on one of his out-of-the-body experiences, Strieber came into the presence of his father, who had been dead for many years.

Strieber also saw the visitors stacking up gray boxes, which he associated with coffins. They weren't coffins, really, but they seemed to have some connection to physical death—or at least to the passage of the soul from this lifetime into the next.

If there is one thing the visitors have brought to Whitley Strieber it is the assurance that the human soul does exist, that it can operate independently of the physical body, and that it will live on beyond the grave.

Strieber understands that these creatures, whatever their connection with death, operate primarily in the spiritual realm and that they seem to have some sort of connection to the afterlife.

"Not only are we not alone, we have a life in another form—and it is on that level of reality that the visitors are primarily present."[8]

Some people are convinced that the visitors have come here to assist us. Stumbling blindly along on our own, we are drawing dangerously close to global destruction. But the visitors have come to help us confront the peril and overcome it. It's dark as midnight all about us, but working hand-in-hand with the visitors we'll soon see the morning sun breaking through.

That sort of talk gives me a very uneasy feeling.

The Pied Piper played beautiful music, and the children of Hamlin followed him happily out of the city never to be seen again. That was only a fairy tale, of course, but we can learn from it. Maybe the Pied Piper really did exist. Maybe he still exists today, only in a different form.

I'm not the only one getting an uneasy feeling about the visitors.

Some who have encountered the visitors feel the same way. One woman said she moved to the city to be where there were bright lights, constant noise, and the

---

8. Strieber, *Transformation*, 201.

hustle and bustle of human activity. She believed that the aliens were less likely to get to her if there were other people nearby who might hear her calls for help.

Another woman told UFO researcher Budd Hopkins that she sleeps with a 100-watt light bulb burning in her bedroom lamp. This is no childish fear of the dark. The woman is forty years old, but she has encountered the visitors and feels they are less likely to come into her home if she always has a light on.

Jesus said, "Everyone who does evil hates the light, and will not come into the light for fear that his deeds will be exposed" (John 3:20).

Other abductees, contactees, or whatever you want to call them, report that they have been plagued with terrible nightmares about the strange beings. If it's love and understanding they seek to bring to us, why are they leaving their "chosen ones" in such a state?

Numerous references throughout the Bible tell of human beings coming into contact with angels. I don't presume to know what angels look like because I have never seen one. But I suspect they look nothing at all like they've been portrayed by artists over the centuries.

They don't look like chubby little children with wings or like beautiful, feminine men. Angels apparently are awesome, frightening creatures. Nearly every time the Bible records that a human being encountered an angel, the first words out of the angel's mouth were "Fear not."

The angels knew their appearance would be frightening to an ordinary human being, so they immediately

WHERE ARE THEY TAKING US?

allayed any fear. The Apostle John tells us that "perfect love drives out fear" (1 John 4:18).

In contrast, the visitors leave behind them a trail of sorrow, anger, and fear.

THE ALIEN SCHOOL OF HARD KNOCKS

As mentioned before, many UFO investigators have followed a path that has taken them directly into the world of the occult. They believe they are rediscovering ancient spiritual truths and uncovering new realities about the universe. It's more likely that they are getting involved with some ancient deceptions.

Whitley Strieber was sitting in his upstate New York cabin one evening when he heard a series of sharp knocking sounds coming from the outside wall. Each of three series of knocks consisted of three loud raps. The noises were so rhythmic and so strong that it sounded as if they were being produced by a machine. The noise scared Strieber's cats half to death. They both ran from the room in a terror, and one did not emerge from its hiding place in the linen closet until twenty-four hours later.

In the days just before this experience, Strieber had been wondering why the visitors always came to him in the middle of the night. It was always like a dream and yet it wasn't a dream. He wanted something to let him know that this whole thing was real and not just a projection of his mind.

Then came the loud rappings on the cabin wall that were real enough to send the cats into a panic.

WHERE ARE THEY TAKING US?

Over the next few weeks Strieber tried everything possible to duplicate those noises without success. But during all of his experiments the cats weren't frightened at all. They slept peacefully.

Strieber said the rapping noises he heard were nothing at all like those in spiritualist seances because they were more rhythmic and more forceful. It seems he was trying to distance himself from the sort of thing that has been occurring in the medium's parlor for many years. But that's not so easy to do because "spirits of the dead" have been announcing themselves in this way ever since the spiritualist phenomena began to catch on in the middle of the nineteenth century.

Rappings and tappings have long been considered one of the primary forms of communication between this world and the next, a sort of supernatural Morse code. What's more, such rappings have been a consistent feature of hauntings and poltergeistic activities.

If there is no connection between Strieber's visitors and the spirit world, why did they choose the same method to demonstrate their reality? *[margin note: Dubious inference]*

Bangings and rappings were among the ways the spiritual entities contacted by the medium Ben Alexander made their presence known to him. These "spirits" were kind and encouraging as long as Alexander listened to them and obeyed their leading without question. But as soon as he began to have second thoughts about the whole business they turned against him with a vengeance, threatening to destroy him if he didn't comply with their wishes. Whoever was in contact with

Ben Alexander saw him as an entrance into our world and wasn't about to give up that "port of entry" without a battle.

Alexander's experiences were parallelled by those of French medium Raphael Gasson, who also became convinced that he was not in touch with benevolent beings from "the other side," but rather with malevolent entitities who used every deceitful trick they could to gain control over human minds and souls. His story was told in the book *The Challenging Counterfeit*, published by Logos International.

The spiritualist landscape is strewn with the wreckage of men and women who thought they were in touch with kindly spirit guides, or even with departed loved ones, only to find that the whole thing was a screen for vicious supernatural forces.

The Bible tells us, in the Book of Revelation, that Jesus Christ stands at the door and knocks, waiting for us to open our hearts and receive Him. But someone else is standing at the door of our world and knocking. Knocking very loudly, in fact. And experience reveals that he's not the sort of person to whom we want to open the door.

FOOTSTEPS IN THE DARK

Whitley Strieber's search for the truth about his visitors eventually led him to Wisconsin's Circle Sanctuary, a retreat owned by the Wiccan religion. Wicca is also known as witchcraft, but Strieber claims it has "no relationship to Satanism or other such perversions," and that it is a Western version of shamanism, "which is the oldest of all human religious traditions."

Shamanism, according to the *Encyclopedia International,* is a religion that claims "to have direct intercourse with the spirits pervading the world. . . . The shaman acts as a medium, and modern spiritualism may have its roots in ancient Asiatic shamanistic practices.

"The North American shaman, often called medicine man or conjurer, as among the Ojibwa of northern United States and Canada, works through familiar spirits, who visit him in a specially constructed lodge."

On a moonlit June night, Strieber stood in a circle with two friends on the property of Circle Sanctuary preparing to begin one of Wicca's religious ceremonies. Before they began, they heard footsteps. Although they couldn't see anyone, they called out a greeting anyway, asking whoever was approaching to take part in the ceremony.

There was no reply, except for the sound of the footsteps coming closer to the circle. The footsteps stopped for a minute. After a few seconds of silence, the invisible being resumed its walk, moving away from the group and apparently right over the edge of a cliff. Then, as the three began their ceremony, they heard the sounds of footsteps all around them. But they never saw anyone at all. Later that night, two other people reported strange occurrences near the sanctuary. One had seen a lighted disk-shaped object flying through the sky. The other reported a ball of fire bouncing along the ground.

Did the aliens bring Strieber into contact with Wicca and the Circle Sanctuary, or did they merely follow him there? Given the experiences of others, it seems likely that they were the inspiration behind his involvement with such spiritualistic practices.

Al Bender, who wrote the book about his encounter with the three men in black, also heard footsteps in his house after he became interested in the mystery of UFOs. He would awaken during the night and hear someone approaching his bedroom. The sound of human footsteps came down the hall and stopped just outside the door. Bender would sneak across the room and wait behind the door, ready to grab the intruder as he came through. But nobody ever did. Finally Bender would throw open the door himself, prepared to tackle whoever was standing in the hall. But there was no one there.

After a while, he became used to the sound of footsteps when nobody was there. He knew there weren't any intruders—at least of the human variety.

Whitley Strieber has come to believe there is some connection between the ancient religions and the appearance of his visitors. He engages in Wicca rituals, celebrates the "harmonic convergence," and expresses his hope "that the world would come to see Native Americans, Australians, Africans, and other ancient peoples as the precious and threatened sources of wisdom and guidance that they really are."[9]

---

9. Strieber, *Transformation*, 235.

Ancient humans believed there were spirits lurking everywhere—in trees, under rocks, behind bushes, in streams—you name it and there was a spirit involved. They had to walk with extreme caution because they didn't want to risk offending any of those spirits, and they were forever making sacrifices in an effort to appease them.

In his book *Eternity in Their Hearts*, Don Richardson does an excellent job of showing how true religion—the worship of the one true God, Creator of heaven and earth—degenerated into shamanism.

Shamanism is an ancient religion, yes, but that doesn't make it any less a corruption of the truth. The same spirits who sought to draw people away from the truth thousands of years ago are still active in the world today. When it comes to religion, very few ancient truths are waiting to be rediscovered, only ancient deceptions waiting to be dusted off and given a thin coat of 1990s varnish.

Eventually Strieber comes to the point of complete trust in the visitors. In one of his most terrifying statements, he writes:

> What is interesting to me now is how to develop effective techniques to call them [the visitors] into one's life and make use of what they have to offer. I have described gross versions of such techniques, such as developing real questions and being willing to be taken on a journey through one's fears. The most effective technique seems to be simply to open oneself, asking for what one needs

the most without placing any conditions at all on what they might be.[10]

He seems to believe he can summon the visitors at will, almost as if he can control them.

The Satanists, with their pentagrams and magic circles, believe they can summon the inhabitants of the spirit world at will. They believe they can control the demons and get them to do their bidding. It just doesn't work that way. A demon may seem to obey for a while, but he always knows that he controls the situation.

There are indeed a number of connections between the visitors and the world of spiritism. The visitor experience goes hand in hand with involvement in the occult, witchcraft, and other facets of the New Age movement. And it has led many to experiment with astral projection, to believe in reincarnation, and to get involved in other practices that directly oppose the historic teachings of the Christian church.

The plain truth is that the visitors, whoever and whatever they may be, have not left behind a legacy of light and understanding. Instead, they've left a trail of confusion and sorrow.

---

10. Strieber, *Transformation*, 236.

Chapter Eight

WHO IS LORD OF THIS UNIVERSE?

On July 2, 1947, startling news came out of Roswell, New Mexico. A flying saucer had crashed on a ranch near town, and air force personnel were on the scene.

In 1947 the horrors of World War II were still very much on the minds of every American, and so the sight of huge metallic disks zipping through our nation's skies caused much uneasiness.

Some speculated that the disks might be a secret weapon developed by the Nazis or the Japanese near the end of the war. Maybe our enemies had not been completely defeated and were looking for the opportunity to launch a surprise attack.

Others guessed that the flying saucers had been developed by the United States for use during the war, but had not been perfected in time. Quite a bit of top secret work was going on in New Mexico at the time—at Los Alamos and White Sands—so it made sense to believe the saucers had something to do with it.

There was also speculation that the saucers had come from another planet. Alarmed by our warlike tendencies, they were spying on our military installations.

The crash at Roswell made big news. The air force assured the public that a top intelligence officer, Major Jesse Marcel, was on the scene and that his report would be released to the public just as soon as possible. Less than twenty-four hours later, the announcement came.

False alarm, the air force said. The crashed saucer had been a weather balloon.

Some people believed the official explanation, but many more did not. There were rumors that the air force had bullied the rancher into keeping his mouth shut about the incident. According to some reports he was even jailed for a few days to get him to rethink what had happened on his property.

It's unclear whether or not this really occurred, but rumors spread rapidly across the country, adding fuel to the speculation that the air force was hiding something of gigantic proportions.

It was even said that the air force had run all sorts of tests on the crashed saucer and had come to the conclusion that it was not constructed from any metals available on earth.

Even bigger news was that several small bodies had been removed from the crash site and were being examined by military doctors. The biggest news of all was that one or more of these "space invaders" may have been captured and were being held by the United States government.

In the years since the Roswell incident, the controversy has not gone away.

An "official" letter has been circulated claiming to prove that the air force covered up the true nature of the incident. Some "authorities" have denounced the letter as a forgery. Other "experts" have said there is no reason to doubt its authenticity. It has all the earmarks of an official document, they say.

In a 1979 documentary titled *Flying Saucers Are Real*, Major Marcel finally spoke openly about his investigation into the saucer crash. He said,

> One thing I was certain of, being familiar with all air activities, was that it was not a weather balloon, not an aircraft, or a missile. . . . A lot of the little members had little symbols which we were calling hieroglyphics because they couldn't be read. . . .
>
> The reason this story has remained hidden from the public for over thirty years is that General Rainey released a cover story at that point.[1]

In 1987, a paper surfaced that was said to have been written for President Harry Truman, explaining the incident to him. This paper said there had been not one crash of a flying disk, but several in different parts of

---

1. Quoted in Strieber, *Transformation*, 118.

the southwestern United States, and that there had been at least one survivor. He was referred to as Ebe, for "extraterrestrial biological entity." The report said that Ebe eventually died of unknown causes.

The story of Ebe surfaced again in 1988 when a syndicated television special on the UFO phenomenon interviewed a man who claimed to be a former intelligence officer with firsthand knowledge of the case.

Appearing on "UFO Coverup," hosted by actor Mike Farrell, the man said there had been more than one survivor of such crashes, and that one was still in the custody of the U.S. government. He was not really a prisoner, the man said, but rather a guest. We were not holding him against his will; he was stranded here.

The producers of the special told viewers they had examined the man's credentials, and they seemed to be in order. But the man remained in the shadow and his voice was electronically distorted when he told of his long association with Ebe. He implied that it would be dangerous for him to identify himself. (That's always the way it is with the flying saucer stories. Either everything is top secret, to the point that those who know the truth are afraid to tell it, or the evidence disappears before it can be shown to the public.)

He talked at some length regarding Ebe's biological and psychological makeup, and then he was asked if the extraterrestrial believed in any sort of religion.

Yes, as a matter of fact, he replied, Ebe was a deeply religious being, although he didn't seem to worship a Supreme Being. It was more like he worshiped the universe. He seemed to believe that the universe itself was God, and he had a complete reverence for the cosmos.

Implanted in all humans is a spiritual longing. We all want to know why we are here, what is the ultimate meaning of life, and we long to know about God and eternity. And if a spaceman knows enough about the physical universe to travel billions of miles to reach earth, we think surely we can trust him when he talks about spiritual things.

Upon hearing him say, "Our God is the universe," millions of people will discard what they perceive to be antiquated ideas about God, and grab onto this new religion for all they're worth.

If someone wanted to sweep out the old religions and bring in a new one, he or she could hardly do better than to have the new religion endorsed by a being from outer space.

Whitley Strieber appears to long for us to return to the wisdom of shamanism—a religion that worships spirits residing in rocks, trees, rivers, and lakes. Really, shamanism is the worship of the creation—and so of the universe.

And now, hundreds of years later, the spokesman for Ebe tells us that space beings worship the universe, a newer and higher form of shamanism, but shamanism just the same.

Primitive man may have bowed down before volcanos and prayed to the sun, moon, or stars—and modern man thinks how ignorant he was to worship these inanimate objects. But then along come space beings who tell us they worship the universe, and we see it as the deepest sort of wisdom.

The Bible tells us that when people first began to stray from the worship of the true God, they began to worship the things they saw around them—birds, animals, mountains. People had a hard time staying loyal to God because they couldn't see God, and they wanted to worship something they could see. They needed an image to hold in mind, and it was impossible to hold an image of the invisible and eternal.

And so the forces of deception at work in the world led them to worship the creation instead of the Creator.

We haven't advanced much in the past few thousand years; today we are confronted on all sides with the notion that our allegiance belongs to the universe itself, rather than to the One who created it.

And Ebe—whether or not he really existed—was among the prophets of this message.

The Apostle Paul spoke to this: "They exchanged the truth of God for a lie, and worshiped and served created things rather than the Creator—who is forever praised" (Romans 1:25).

He also said, "Furthermore, since they did not think it worthwhile to retain the knowledge of God, he gave them over to a depraved mind, to do what ought not to be done" (Romans 1:28).

The more we know about the universe, the more we are inspired to worship. As we learn about the vastness of space, the billions of stars and planets, and as we see the way it all fits together, we are filled with awe. But that awe should be directed not at the universe itself, but at the One who made it—who thought it all up and then put it together.

UFO literature is filled with the idea that our universe is alive and that it deserves, if not worship, at least respect and reverence.

One of Ruth Montgomery's space friends—even though he's an earthling in this incarnation—explains that the universe is like the human body. He likens the stars and planets and the spaces between them to the protons, neutrons, and electrons within the atom. He writes:

> We must realize that the distance between the atoms in our bodies (atoms being building blocks of all matter) is exactly proportional to the distance between the stars. In other words, if we take two atoms and multiply them to the size of stars, the ratio of the distances between is the same. But when we observe the life in our bodies, where does it exist? Only in the heart? Or brain? Or lungs? Of course not. Life is present everywhere in our bodies. That is why if someone touches any part of your body you can feel it. Now, do you limit the life in your bodies to a cell or an organ? Or do you say that life is a universalized presence in the body? It is, upon thinking, universalized. . . .
>
> Taking this concept to the next logical conclusion, is it so difficult to realize that since the relative distances between atoms and between stars are

the same, that life permeates interstellar spaces as it does the interatomic spaces?[2]

Mrs. Montgomery's spirit guides assured her that this was all true.

It's not only in occultic circles that this sort of thought is being promulgated.

Scientist, social critic, and author Jeremy Rifkin believes that science, more and more, is beginning to look upon the universe as an intelligent mechanism. The more science discovers about genetic engineering, for instance, the more it is having to discard some of its long-cherished beliefs.

In his book *Algeny: The Last Magic*, Rifkin reports that scientists have taken some genes from an insect's leg. Then they removed one of the creature's antennas, grafted the leg genes where the antenna had been, and waited to see if the insect would sprout a leg on its head. According to all their knowledge of genes and chromosomes, this is what should have happened.[3]

But it didn't.

Instead, those "leg genes" transformed themselves into a new antenna.

Nothing earthshaking about that? Yes there was, because there was nothing in the genetic code of that leg to give it the "ability" to transform itself into an

---

2. Montgomery, *Aliens Among Us*, 168.
3. Jeremy Rifkin, *Algeny: The Last Magic* (New York: Viking Press, 1983).

WHO IS LORD OF THIS UNIVERSE?

antenna. According to everything the scientists understood, it shouldn't have happened.

Then why did it? Because there is an order and an intelligence at work in the universe that made it happen.

Does that mean we're talking about God?

There aren't many scientists who have room for the word *God* in their vocabularies. Some have concluded that there is an intelligence to the universe itself. There is a grand design to the cosmos, but they still say it all occurred by chance.

Rifkin explains that science is forever modeling its understanding of the universe according to current social conditions.

The industrial revolution of Darwin's day gave rise to a brutality that manifested itself in a financial climate in which only the strong survived. Very often the rich got richer and the poor got poorer, and it truly was a "dog-eat-dog" world. Darwin took those principles, applied them to nature, and came up with the idea of evolution based on the survival of the fittest.

Today, the industrial revolution is long past and we are in the middle of an information revolution. Computers are everywhere, and even children in the primary grades of school have a wealth of information available to them at the touch of a few keys on a keyboard.

Because of that, many of today's scientists have come to see the universe as one gigantic computer. Anything we want to know is accessible almost immediately, if we know the correct buttons to push. Information is swirling all about us, and it occasionally produces some amazing results—but, they tell us, that doesn't mean there's really a Mind behind it. After all, there is no real intelligence to a computer. It's just a machine. But it took someone with a mind and a soul to create that computer.

All around us are evidences of God's wisdom and power, but millions of people can't see God because their eyes are so full of the things He created.

To put it as simply as possible, there are forces at work in this universe of ours that don't want us to have anything to do with God. These forces will do whatever it takes to get us to take our eyes off Him—and one of the oldest tricks in their book is to get people to focus attention on the creation instead of the Creator.

THEY FELL FROM HEAVEN

According to Scripture, a rebellion occurred eons ago within the ranks of the angels. As many as one-third of the heavenly beings, led by a mighty angel named Lucifer, openly defied God.

Lucifer and his supporters were defeated, but not annihilated. Their judgment is not yet complete, and until the final day comes they are free to roam the universe, doing what they can to entice the created beings of the cosmos to join them in their rebellion.

Some humans acknowledge the presence of Lucifer's band and openly join in the revolt, but others have to be deceived into believing they represent truth and good.

WHO IS LORD OF THIS UNIVERSE?

Christianity is not the only religion that teaches the existence of demons, or fallen angels.

According to Persian and Chaldean tradition, the fallen angels, or the Ahrimanes, occupy the part of the universe between the earth and the stars, a land called Ahrimane-Abad.

Trevor James Constable, a military and aviation historian and author of several books, tells in *The Battle for the Earth* that he has come to the conclusion that Ahrimanic powers are seeking to gain control of the earth by weakening us from within, rather than without. What's more, they have come to us through inner space, rather than outer space.

Twenty-five or thirty years ago, people who believed in flying saucers were convinced they came from a nearby planet or a neighboring solar system. But the more we know about our universe, the less likely this seems.

Whitley Strieber's visitors are often accompanied by balls of light and flying disks, but he has slowly come to the conclusion that they do not come from Zeta Reticuli or anywhere else within our known physical universe. It's more likely, he says, that they come from another dimension—perhaps an unseen world that parallels ours. Yes, they have physical characteristics. Strieber knows this because he has touched them. But that doesn't mean they are not primarily spiritual in nature.

We really don't know very much about the spiritual realm. We don't know how it interacts with our physical world or how spiritual beings gain access into our three-dimensional world. But the Bible itself includes accounts of angels eating food and doing other things that indicate they too can be quite physical.

We've always thought that spiritual beings were ephemeral, wispy, transparent creatures. Maybe we've had it all wrong.

If the visitors really are the fallen angels, or if they are working in tandem with those fallen angels, it's our souls they're after, not the planet itself.

The presence of visitors on our planet is nothing new. Even in the Middle Ages there were reports of people encountering unusual beings. Some people claimed to have been taken aboard strange machines and given rides through the heavens. The people who had those experiences usually didn't get to tell very much about them; they were quickly condemned as heretics and witches and put to death.

I'm not advocating a return to those days. Nor do I believe that anyone encountered by a visitor is guilty of hobnobbing with demons.

The Bible tells us that the devil goes about like a roaring lion seeking whom he might devour. If I'm walking through the wilderness and a lion starts chasing me, I haven't done anything wrong. It's the lion's nature to chase his prey. It is, however, up to me to exercise some caution. If I know where the man-eating lions hang out, I'll do myself a favor and stay away from that place.

JESUS CHRIST IS LORD

Has anyone ever told you that Christianity is outdated? It isn't. Have you heard anyone say that Jesus Christ was a wonderful Teacher but that His message became corrupted over the years? He was, but it hasn't. He no doubt was the greatest Teacher who ever lived, and He taught that He was the only Son of God and that faith in Him was necessary for salvation. That was the message He brought two thousand years ago, and that's the same message being preached by the Christian church today. Anything else you hear, whether it comes from visitors, angels, or a professor with a dozen Ph.D.s, simply isn't true.

The Bible says, "Dear friends, do not believe every spirit, but test the spirits to see whether they are from God, because many false prophets have gone out into the world. This is how you can recognize the Spirit of God: Every spirit that acknowledges that Jesus Christ has come in the flesh is from God, but every spirit that does not acknowledge Jesus is not from God" (1 John 4:1–3).

If the visitors acknowledge the Lordship of Christ, we can begin to trust them in other matters. If they don't acknowledge Christ, we can't. That's the simple truth.

Jesus Christ is not only the Lord of this world—He is the Lord of the entire universe. There is evidence for it all around us. Jesus Christ is touching people and changing lives today, just as He did when He walked this planet in the flesh some two thousand years ago.

Christian churches are full of people whose lives have been changed through an encounter with the risen Christ.

WHO IS LORD OF THIS UNIVERSE?

People who have met the visitors will tell you that they too have been changed—but an encounter with these beings and the changes it brings cannot compare to an encounter with Christ and the changes He brings. Consider the evidence:

Penny Tabor. Her neck was broken in an automobile accident and she lived in severe pain for ten years. Doctors could do little to give her relief and advised her that she would have to live with it. One night in desperation she cried out to Jesus Christ. She felt something touch her and then realized that she was totally pain free. She was healed through the touch of Christ.

Felix Barboto. He had cancer of the thorax. Doctors said it was terminal; the cancer had spread too far for them to help him. They sent him home to die. At his sister's request, he attended a healing service at her church. He really didn't have anything to lose, he figured. During the few days following the service, he began to feel better and stronger. His appetite returned. When he went back to his doctor for tests, the amazed physician found that every trace of the cancer had disappeared—without medical help.

Tom Jones. He was an alcoholic whose habit was destroying his family and pushing him toward an early grave. Tom knew he had to do something before it was too late. He remembered the name of a woman who had once tried to counsel him. He decided to give her a call. He went to a pay phone, looked up her number in the book, and was surprised to discover that her name and number were underlined. He called her, and she asked him if he would surrender his life and his problem to Jesus Christ. After agreeing that this was exactly what he wanted and needed to do, Tom prayed with this caring woman—and his desire for alcohol was completely taken away from him.

Pat Terrell. She had a heart condition that kept her in pain and out of breath. The smallest amount of exercise could prove fatal. But she too was prayed for in the name of Jesus Christ, and her heart became healthy and strong.

Marilyn Ford. She was totally blind from a genetic eye disease. Even though she was a strong Christian, married to a minister, and had prayed many times for a healing, it had not come. She tried her best to be satisfied with her life, but she sometimes fell into despair, especially when she thought about never seeing her husband's face. One night her husband decided to pray yet another time for her eyesight to be restored. He fell to his knees beside their bed and began to pray while Marilyn instinctively closed her eyes—as she did every time she prayed. When her husband said "amen," she opened her eyes, as she had done countless times before. But this time she could see perfectly.

Do these cases sound too good to be true? Every one is true, and every one is documented. Marilyn Ford has statements from her doctors saying she was blind. Today, she has twenty-twenty vision. Her illness was not psychosomatic; there were physical reasons why she could not see. In fact, when she went to the doctor after her healing, he just shook his head and said he didn't know how she could see. Her eyes were still as damaged as they had ever been; she shouldn't be able to see a thing. Yet she described in detail every item he held in front of her.

If someone said to an unbeliever, "Jesus Christ is the Lord of the universe," that simple statement might be hard to believe. But it's easier to believe when you consider what He has done for Penny Tabor, Felix Barboto, Tom Jones, Pat Terrell, Marilyn Ford, and thousands of others.

If we start with the assumption that Jesus is Lord, that leaves us with a clear choice regarding the visitors. If they lead toward Christ, we can follow them. If they lead away from Christ, we can't afford to follow them.

Furthermore, if we come to the point where we realize that we need to pay attention to the Bible when it tells us about Jesus, shouldn't we also listen when it tells us to avoid involvement in occultic practices?

Consider 2 Thessalonians 2:11, which says that God sometimes sends a "powerful delusion" to those who will not believe the truth, so that they might believe a lie. Jesus Himself says that "false Christs and false prophets will appear and perform great signs and miracles to deceive even the elect—if that were possible" (Matthew 24:24). And the Apostle John also writes, "Many deceivers . . . have gone out into the world" (2 John 7).

There were deceivers then, and there are deceivers now. Things have changed, but things stay the same.

Please don't think I'm saying there is no such thing as life on other planets. I don't know whether there is or isn't, but it wouldn't surprise me if there is. God isn't wasteful, and since He created all the planets and stars of the universe, it wouldn't surprise me at all if He put living creatures on many of them. God created all the living creatures, and it wouldn't hurt my faith a single bit if a flying saucer landed on the White House lawn one of these days. But my faith in Christ would take precedence over anything the space being might say.

Jesus says, "I am the good shepherd; I know my sheep and my sheep know me—just as the Father knows me and I know the Father—and I lay down my life for the sheep. I have other sheep that are not of this sheep pen. I must bring them also. They too will listen to my voice, and there shall be one flock and one shepherd" (John 10:14–16).

This passage has been quoted from time to time by those who believe the "Jesus is an alien" theory. They believe these "other sheep" are those who live on other planets.

I seriously doubt that this is the case. It seems apparent from the context of this and other passages that Jesus is referring to the door of salvation that opened to the Gentiles. If there are humanlike creatures on other planets, and if they have been given indwelling spirits, be assured that the wise among them will be sheep in the Good Shepherd's flock.

The Bible has plenty to say about the message the visitors are bringing to our planet:

WHO IS LORD OF THIS UNIVERSE?

1. Salvation will not come down from the stars.

Throughout the Bible, God makes the point again and again. If we look anywhere other than to Him for salvation and security, we are looking in the wrong places. Science won't save us. Technology won't save us. Love won't save us. Universal peace won't save us.

There is one God, and He holds the universe in His hands. If we look to Him for our salvation, we will not be disappointed. If we look anywhere else, we will be not only disappointed, but enslaved as well.

The salvation and redemption of planet earth will be found in God and God alone.

2. You cannot find God by looking within yourself.

One of the most popular messages the visitors are bringing our way is that God is in all of us. It's a message repeated over and over in the various aspects of the New Age religions. "I am God, you are God, he is God, she is God," they say.

Sorry, but it just isn't true. You're not God, and neither am I. There is one God, and He is on His throne in heaven.

The Bible teaches that human beings are made in God's image. It also tells us that God gave us a spirit, so there is something of the supernatural within us—but that doesn't mean we are little versions of God.

The New Testament teaches that when a person is born again, when he or she surrenders to Christ, the Holy Spirit comes to live within that person. In this way,

WHO IS LORD OF THIS UNIVERSE?

it is possible to have God's presence within us, but it is not the same as having always had God within us and simply having to find the part of ourselves that is divine.

Unless we have surrendered our lives to God through Jesus Christ, we will not be able to look within ourselves and find God.

In the Bible's account of how sin entered the world, Satan appeared to Eve and talked her into eating the fruit from the tree of knowledge of good and evil. God had told Adam and Eve they would die if they ate of that fruit, but Satan disagreed. In effect he told them, "God knows that if you eat of the fruit you'll become wise, just like He is. That's why He doesn't want you to do it."

So man's first temptation was to see himself as a small version of God. We're still making that mistake today, thinking we can be a little god if only we focus on the divinity that lies within us.

The serpent came to Eve and said, "You and Adam can be like God."

The visitors come to us and say, "You can be God-like."

It's the same old story in a different disguise.

3. There is a spirit world.

Humanly speaking, our experiences are limited to what we can register through the five senses. But there are many things in the physical world that we know exist even though we can't see them. We can't see electricity, for instance, but we don't doubt its existence. In fact, we have become so dependent on it that most of us don't know what to do when a storm knocks the power off. We can't see ultraviolet rays in the sunlight, but we certainly feel their effects if we spend too much time at the beach on a sunny summer day.

The spiritual universe parallels these phenomena in that we can't normally see it, hear it, or perceive it with any of our senses. That isn't to say, though, that no spiritual beings ever cross back and forth between the two "realities."

The Bible says there are principalities and powers within this spiritual realm. Angels and demons exist in this realm, and apparently so do the dead. Although the dead seem to be separated from the earth—remember that the Bible warns against trying to contact them—the angels and demons apparently can move back and forth from one realm of existence to the other.

When Jesus Christ ascended into heaven, His apostles watched Him rise into the skies. He might just as well have ascended sideways, however, since He was being taken into the spiritual realm of existence.

It's not chic, here in the closing years of the twentieth century, to believe in evil spirits, but the Bible says they exist. Jesus Christ acknowledged their existence, cast them out of many possessed people, and warned against being fooled by them.

Beings from the spirit world may show themselves to us, and they can also give us visions, enable us to hear disembodied voices, and play all sorts of strange tricks on us.

Our vantage point gives us the impression that we live in the "real" universe, and that the spiritual realm is a sort of shadowland. It exists, yes, but not in the way we understand existence. But Jesus taught that obtaining abundant life in the spiritual realm is worth any sacrifice a person could possibly make in the physical realm. That indicates that truth is opposite from what we usually think. Actually, it's the physical universe that is the shadowy half-life, and we won't be truly alive until we have "passed over" to the spiritual plane.

[margin note: really?]

Those who don't believe that the spiritual universe exists have only one explanation for the visitors—they come from another planet. However, if we acknowledge the existence of the spiritual universe, as Christ did, that opens all sorts of possibilities relating to the true nature of these alien beings.

4. Beware of listening to anyone who wants to lead you into the occult.

The Bible says that those who visit mediums, consult familiar spirits, and get involved with witchcraft or any other similar activity are in rebellion against God.

Almost inevitably, a deep interest in UFOs leads to involvement in occultic practices, and this is especially true of those who have experienced "contact."

Involvement in the occult is flat-out dangerous. Spirits will come to you as if they are your friends, as if they want to open up the gates of knowledge and allow you to come inside—but all they really want is to control you—body, mind, and soul.

Many years ago, a pretty, intelligent girl got involved in a serious way with the Ouija board. Helen's mother had died at a very young age, and the girl was devastated. But through her Ouija board, she believed she had reestablished contact with her mother. She couldn't wait to get home from school every day to "talk" to her.

Before too long, these conversations with her mother were her primary reason for living. She and her mother hadn't been that close when the woman was alive, but now they were inseparable. What's more, "Mom" was extremely possessive. She demanded all of her daughter's time, cutting her off from her friends and giving her lessons in various occultic arts.

Helen's friends began to leave her alone, her grades dropped drastically, and she always looked tired and haggard. She had all the symptoms of drug addiction, but it wasn't drugs she was addicted to. It was the occult.

I lost contact with her for several years, and then one day I ran into her on the street. She looked ten years older than she was, told me she was getting by on welfare because she couldn't find a decent job, and admitted that her life was a mess.

I'm not saying that everyone who has ever experimented with the Ouija board has wound up in Helen's condition, nor am I saying that Helen's problems all stemmed from her involvement in the occult. But I saw firsthand the changes her involvement produced, and I believe that was where her downfall began.

Involvement in the occult is every bit as dangerous

WHO IS LORD OF THIS UNIVERSE?

as involvement with the most addictive drugs—no matter what the visitors might say.

   5. *There's a war going on out there.*

Remember the words of the Apostle Paul:

> For our struggle is not against flesh and blood, but against the rulers, against the authorities, against the powers of this dark world and against the spiritual forces of evil in the heavenly realms. Therefore put on the full armor of God, so that when the day of evil comes, you may be able to stand your ground....
>
> Ephesians 6:12, 13

   The Bible teaches that a rebellion occurred way back in the far distant past. Satan thought he could do a better job of running the universe than God was doing, and he convinced a number of other spiritual beings to join his revolt. Although Satan and his followers don't have a chance of winning the war, they have yet to lay down their arms and surrender.

   In other words, there are good guys and bad guys out there. And the bad guys are engaged in guerrilla warfare. They'll do anything they can to win the battle. There are no "rules of war" in this combat.

   What's more, the bad guys have their propaganda machine running at full speed and would love nothing better than for you to believe a few of their lies.

   Whose side are you on?

   Maybe you're still undecided. Or maybe you haven't made a strong commitment to the side of the angels.

WHO IS LORD OF THIS UNIVERSE?

Be assured then, that the bad guys will do everything they can to win you over—and they don't give up easily. One thing they'll never do, though, is reveal their true nature to you.

They won't say, "Hey, we're the bad guys. Want to be on our side?" If they did, they'd get a few folks from the lunatic fringe, but that would be it.

Satan and his followers always present themselves as being on the side of personal freedom, open-mindedness, and human dignity. But they aren't really in favor of any of those ideals.

And when visitors tell someone that all is peace and love everywhere in the universe except here on the earth, they are lying.

6. There is no substitute for the cross of Christ.

The visitors claim to "recycle souls," implying that part of their job is to help us make the transition from this life to the next.

But that's not what Scripture teaches. The Bible says:

> God so loved the world that he gave his one and only Son, that whoever believes in him shall not perish but have eternal life.... Whoever believes in him is not condemned, but whoever does not believe stands condemned already because he has not believed in the name of God's one and only Son.   John 3:16, 18

Dozens of passages throughout the Bible point to the importance of giving Christ control of your life:

WHO IS LORD OF THIS UNIVERSE?

If you confess with your mouth, "Jesus is Lord," and believe in your heart that God raised him from the dead, you will be saved. For it is with your heart that you believe and are justified, and it is with your mouth that you confess and are saved. As the Scripture says, "Anyone who trusts in him will never be put to shame." Romans 10:9–11

No one who denies the Son has the Father; whoever acknowledges the Son has the Father also.
1 John 2:23

For by one offering he has perfected for all time those who are sanctified. Hebrews 10:14 NAS

And Jesus Himself said:

I am the way and the truth and the life. No one comes to the Father except through me.
John 14:6

I am the resurrection and the life. He who believes in me will live, even though he dies; and whoever lives and believes in me will never die.
John 11:25, 26

All authority in heaven and on earth has been given to me. Therefore go and make disciples of all nations, baptizing them in the name of the Father and of the Son and of the Holy Spirit, and teaching them to obey everything I have commanded you. Matthew 28:18–20

Go into all the world and preach the good news to all creation. Whoever believes and is baptized will

> be saved, but whoever does not believe will be condemned.   Mark 16:15, 16

These are not just words from an ancient book. They are the words of the sovereign God of the universe. Millions of people today can vouch for the changes that occurred in their lives when they surrendered themselves to Jesus Christ.

According to Hebrews:

> Just as man is destined to die once, and after that to face judgment, so Christ was sacrificed once to take away the sins of many people; and he will appear a second time, not to bear sin, but to bring salvation to those who are waiting for him.
>   Hebrews 9:27, 28

Here, as in numerous other passages, the Bible says we have just one life to live. When that life in the flesh ends, we will be judged, and our eternal state in the spiritual realm will depend on the outcome of that judgment.

The visitors' message conflicts with this simple teaching, which is one of the primary beliefs of all Christianity. The visitors say, "Do your best in this life, but don't worry too much if you blow it because you'll get plenty of other chances."

The world of these aliens is not troubled by the Gospel of Christ, and that is perhaps the most troubling thing about them. Christ's entry into our physical world was the most profound event of history, and anyone who brings a message of eternal life and peace that bypasses the incarnation is, to put it bluntly, not to be trusted.

Something is going on out there. Something real. It is not a dream nor a hallucination.

We are not alone in this universe, nor are we alone on this planet.

Strange beings pilot glowing, silver disks through our skies. They come into our houses in the middle of the night and play mind games with us. They take humans aboard their "craft" for physical examinations. And, finally, they try to change our perceptions about life—in both the physical and spiritual sense.

They come to us not with the flutter of angels' wings, but with the whirr and swoosh of the engines of interstellar spacecraft.

In the conclusion of *Transformation*, Whitley Strieber writes that "We will discover truths about ourselves, truths that will change each of us—and all of us—forever. We will pierce the fog that has for so many long years obscured our vision.

"At last, we will see."[4]

There is reason to believe, however, that the visitors will not help us dispel the fog, but lead us deeper into it, until we are hopelessly lost.

"If a blind man leads a blind man, both will fall into a pit" (Matthew 15:14 NAS).

---

4. Strieber, *Transformation*, 243.